Surviving Being Single

Past 40

Living Life Fully

With or Without a Partner

By

Valerie Pederson

Acknowledgement

This book is dedicated to all my friends throughout my life who provided me support, comfort and fodder for this book. I am especially grateful to those who helped me through being single past 40 and provided me their personal experiences. Additional thanks are given to Barbara Horan for all her wonderful editing assistance.

Obtain a CD or cassette tape of the guided relaxations described in this book in one of the following ways:

Go to: www.Surviving-Life-Mindfully.com

Send an email to: SurvivingBooks@aol.com

Write to: Surviving Life Mindfully
           PO Box 254
           Stow, MA 01775

Surviving Being Single Past 40: Living Life Fully, With or Without a Partner
By Valerie Pederson

Preface

I was married when I was 44 years old. Many people might think that a person who marries that "old" does so because they rarely dated or didn't get out much. That certainly was not the case with me. My relatively late marriage was a definite result of a combination of a fear of long term relationships and (at least in my 20's) just not wanting to get married at all.

I kissed my 10th boy on my 16th birthday. Even though I was a tomboy, the boys I hung out with also were into knowing what kissing was about, and so was I. By the time I was 21, I had been proposed to eight times. All of this led me to believe that I could marry when I wanted, and I certainly didn't want to get married before 21. In fact, when I was 22, I saw my future as a fairly routine, dull continuum: Birth –> College –> Marry –> Kids –> Death. I do not know which scared me more, marrying, death or the predictability of it all.

The fear of the life continuum changed by the time I was 28 and had ended (actually he ended) a long term relationship. Suddenly, I felt like an old maid – and my sister (who had married at 19) encouraged that feeling. She would ask who would want me now – and I'd better get married soon, or I'd never have kids.

Hmmph, kids, another thing to think about. I really liked kids, and kids really liked me. Where did kids stand in this picture of getting married? Suddenly, *I* was thinking I should get married soon because (like many people were saying) all the good ones would get taken. I began dating furiously. It was an activity I always abhorred – thinking that it really didn't tell you anything about the person – just a way to pass the time and please family members by being able to say with a smile – "Yes, I'm dating". At 30, I had my next serious fling – with someone 8 years my junior. He made me feel young, energetic and attractive. But, I still wanted a serious relationship and not too long after my fling ended, I found the man I thought fit all the criteria I was looking for: nice looking, taller than I, had been an Eagle Scout, had a good job and came from a good family. What more could I ask for? – OH YAH – that he DIDN'T GET DRUNK MOST EVERY DAY!!!! a minor (not!) fact that I somehow overlooked. Oh, but I was in love and I thought things could work out – after all he had all the other characteristics I wanted. We moved in together and bought a house. Now, I am not one who likes to regrets actions I've taken – but this was the biggest mistake I had ever made in my life. The house became a chain around my neck. A house that my boyfriend kept taking apart in his blackouts and never finding the time to put together when he was sober. By the end of the relationship (which lasted about 6 years) he was cheating on me and the house looked like a hurricane had hit it. I finally asked him to move out and he did – in with his other girl friend.

For the next few years, I went through what I might refer to as my *Crush Years*. One after the other I developed an attraction for a number of inappropriate men. Whenever I had a quiet moment I would dream about this man. I would dwell on how his neck curved so cleanly, or how often he talked to me so sweetly. I would fantasize about how wonderful my life would be – if and only if – he wasn't gay, he would ask me out, or he didn't have a girlfriend – if only. . .

I did try dating. But, that never worked out at all. Finally, I realized (with the help of some dear friends) that the reason I was developing these crushes was because I had been badly hurt in my last relationship. I was afraid to get into another "real" relationship, one where I didn't just daydream about being held romantically, but would really be held in someone's arms. I took this information to heart.

It wasn't long after that, I met Mark, whom I ended up marrying.

Can I say that being married is the be-all and end all? Not quite. Being married is OK, but, sometimes it is a lot of hard work, constant compromising being the biggest thing. The single life was OK, but there were challenges there too: I was lonely a lot. I look back at my life as a single woman and think, I was pretty happy (especially when I wasn't thinking about the man I wasn't dating). If I knew then what I know now, I would have been a lot happier. I wouldn't have obsessed about finding the right man. I wouldn't think about the trips I couldn't take because I didn't have a man. I wouldn't feel embarrassed because I was 40 and still single. A person can be single (divorced or widowed) and be happy at any age – and that is what this book is about.

I believe if you resolve the types of day to day issues, such as the ones described in this book, you will be closer to being centered in your life and wiser in your choice to marry, stay single, and live life fully either way.

I have been a meditator for many years. I have found that positive thinking; affirmations and relaxations helped me maintain a steady attitude. Also, I felt that if every day I did certain activities, then I also felt better. I talked this over with friends and one (a therapist) said that I should write that down and market it.

I hope this book will help you through your single 40's, 50's or whatever age you are as you date, not date, but either way grow as a person.

Introduction

Whether you are single because you never married, are divorced, gay, or widowed, if you are single and over 40 years of age, this can be a difficult time of your life, but you've come to the right place now. This book will teach know how to be a blissful, centered single, living life fully, doing what you want at every turn. Armed with knowledge such as 50% of the population is single, you will discover that you are not alone and do not have to rush into finding a partner and getting married. You are at the right place if you want to thrive and have fun as a single person and learn how to deal with singledom's most difficult issues, such as an unethical mechanic.

Empower yourself by discovering:

- If you want to marry,
- Whom you want to marry, and
- How to find the person you want to marry.

Finally, learn affirmations and meditations that will help you over those single hurdles, such as first dates and rejection from a potential partner.

The surviving book series presents an empowering fivefold process that will help you through somewhat challenging circumstances while making wise choices and discovering the place you want to be. Getting married is a choice. This fact is often forgotten because of the pressure society puts upon us each and every day. We can have both internal and external pressure to get married and have children. Pressure comes from our parents, siblings and society in general. So, how do we overcome this pressure and make the choice to get married or stay single in a mindful way? Let me provide some suggestions, according to the Surviving Life Mindfully process:

- Learn the correct information about single life. If you are sitting at home feeling that you are the only person who is single, then no number of affirmations and meditations will change your mind. But, knowing the fact that 1 in 10 people never marry, and a whopping one quarter of the U.S. population live by themselves may make you not feel so hurried to get a partner.

- See that when you handle situations effectively you feel more empowered in who you are today. If you know how to take out a mortgage or deal successfully with a business scam, you can say to yourself: I can do this on my own. By knowing these facts, you can be more confident in going on with your life (and not wait or need someone to come and help you).

- Become knowledgeable about what makes you happy and how to go for it. Let's say you have always wanted to go to Mozambique, but your feet feel stuck in cement waiting for this trip to occur because you think you must have a partner before getting on the plane. On the other hand, let's say you know the right travel agency who will hook you up with other singles who also want to go to Mozambique. Now you feel less in need of a partner and more able to make your dreams come true.

- Learn how to make an informed decision when looking for a partner. First, complete a chart that contains over 50 characteristics to help you decide what you really want in a mate. Then, find out the different ways to find a mate these days, stay safe while going on those dates and handling rejection (hopefully that won't occur).

- Attain the life you want through deep relaxations and affirmations. The affirmations specifically written for the single person will help you become happier, decide if you want a life partner, and how to deal with the emotions that this all evokes. Guided meditations will help you feel relaxed when you go on that first date, feel empowered even though you just had a relationship end, and deal with the uncertainty you sense when you haven't had a date for awhile.

This optimistic and motivating book arms you with information that will help you decide if being married is really the thing for you. As a single person you will find information that will tell you how you can live life fully. After you do the meditations and affirmations you will come to believe you deserve the best possible life. You will uncover your desires and learn how to go after them.

There is something in this book for those of you who are at a turning point in your life and want to take some time to become self-assured as a single person and conduct a mindful search for your partner. After you read this book, you will never feel out of step as a single person again, instead you will be confident in who you are and what you can be.

Chapter 1   Just the Facts Please

"To understand everything is to forgive everything"

Original Buddha
(Hindu Prince Gautama Siddharta, the founder of Buddhism, 563-483 B.C)

At one time, people died before they reached the age of 40 and married at a young age. Today, the average life expectancy is more than 77 years[i]. Therefore we have more time to make our marital decisions: to have children or not to have children; to marry or not to marry or most any combination of the above. The options close down when we feel society is pressuring us to get married. We feel alone when we look around and (feel like) we see only couples and families in our midst; or when we walk down the street and see babies – and wonder: why am I not married? This chapter will help you get a reality check on who is married and who is having children. As you read through the statistics (mostly gathered from the US Census Bureau) you will realize you are definitely within the norm and discover some rather amazing facts:

- The age that people are first getting married.

- The number of women currently living with their spouse.

- The percentage of marriages that end in divorce and how has that changed over the last 20-30 years.

- The trend towards not having children or having fewer children.

- Special laws that only apply to single people.

You have the choice of how to create your life.

What Describes a Single Person?

For the purposes of this book, the definition of a single person is one who is not currently married. You may be single because you never married, are widowed or are divorced. You may also consider yourself single if you are gay and without a permanent partner. Let me tell you some specific information about singles like you.

Single: Widowed

Since the average life expectancy has grown from about 47 years at the turn of the century to just over 73 for males and just over 79 for females born today, the odds have increased that people will experience the loss of a spouse. While the total percent of widowed persons is 14 percent the percent of the number of men being widowed over the number of women being widowed is staggering: 3 percent of men were widowers while 11 percent of women were widowed [ii]

The death of a spouse hurts deeply, but fewer taboos about dating and remarrying makes widowhood less of an ordeal than in the past.

"When John Kennedy died, many people got mad when Jacqueline Kennedy started dating because they thought she should be a widow for a lot longer time," said the sociologist and expert on widowhood. "Today we're much more receptive to the notion that you have only one life to live, and if you marry someone else, it's great."

Most widows/widowers date other widows/widowers. Recently, an informal poll was taken on a website for widows and widowers. The poll asked widowers: "If you are dating, what is the marital status of your present significant other?" A whopping 78% of the responding widowers in new relationships said that they were dating widows, while 22% were dating single women (including 12% divorcees and 10% single or never been married).

In a study by the US House Ways and Means Committee in May 2005[iii] it was stated that women live longer than men, spend more time in retirement and are widowed more frequently. A typical 65-year-old woman has a 31 percent chance of living to age 90 or older, as compared to only 18 percent for a typical 65-year-old male. Today, nearly 60 percent of older American women are single, with more than 45 percent widowed. In contrast, only 25 percent of elderly men are single.

As for making friends and maintaining casual relationships sociologists agree that men are more likely to be socially isolated, less frequently in touch with children or church activities. Women are much better at making friends and keeping friends.

Younger widows still have their whole lives in front of them. They may have children, which means there is a real economic problem, and it may interfere with dating or with making a premature decision about getting married. Consider this personal experience of my father becoming a widower in 1953.

I think of my father who was a widow at age 34. That was in 1953. He suddenly had three small children, including me, who was an infant. In those days, formalized day care was unheard of, and we three were shuttled from relative to friend. My sister and brother were even placed in an orphanage for a time. I wonder what he thought about dating, or was his mind concerned mostly with taking care of his children and grieving the loss of his wife. Either way, he married my stepmother a year and a half after my mother died. My siblings and I always wonder if he married her only because he wanted a mother for us. Maybe because he married so soon, maybe because he didn't date anyone else, he made, in me and my siblings opinion, a bad decision. But maybe he married my stepmother who was a widow herself. She could understand his grief, and she was someone who could form stability for his young children. My father remained married to her for almost 50 years, until he died in 2004.

The marriage penalty seems to be a determining factor in whether an older widow decides to marry. A marriage penalty exists if two individuals pay higher taxes or receive lower benefits as a married couple than they would if unmarried. Economic theory suggests that by raising the cost of being married, marriage penalties may lead to lower marriage rates. Critics allege that by discouraging marriage, the penalties violate basic principles of equity and efficiency, undermine family values, and negatively affect child outcomes.[iv]

In 1979, there was an increase in the marriage rate of widows 60 or older. This suggests many widows in this age group chose not to marry until the marriage penalty they faced was removed. Also, in the post-1979 period, there was a drop in marriage rates immediately prior to age 60 and an increase after this age. This pattern is not observed in the period before 1979, and nor for divorced women, who generally are not subject to the age-60 remarriage rule. These findings suggest the age-60 remarriage rule affects the timing of marriage and has the most influence on women who are very close to age 60.[v]

Here are some websites that widows and widowers may find helpful:

- **www.widowsource.com/Sex&Dating_content.html:** Contains lots of helpful information for the dating widow and widower.

- **www.ability.org.uk/widows.html:** Contains many links to resources for the widow and widower.

- **www.widownet.org**: An information and self-help resource for, and by, widows and widowers. Topics covered include grief, bereavement, recovery, and other information helpful to people, of all ages, religious backgrounds and sexual orientations, who have suffered the death of a spouse or life partner.

Single: Divorced

Every now and then, the news media will report a new study on the levels of stress caused by various occurrences in our lives, and divorce is always near the top of the list. In fact after the death of a spouse, divorce is the next highest stress event that may occur in one person's life.[vi] In the U.S. alone, there are more than one million divorces a year. That's two million people who have gone through divorce recently. And they all come out of it OK.

Here are some other interesting statistics concerning men and women; divorce and remarriage[vii]:

- In 1998, 59.3 million women were married and 11.1 million women were divorced, compared to 58.6 million men were married and 8.3 million men were divorced.

- The rate for divorce per 1,000 people in 1997 was 4.5, which equaled to 1,163,000 divorces.

- A study done in 2004 informed us that 23 percent of first marriages end in divorce. Of this total one-fifth end within 5 years and one-third end with 10 years.

- Duration of a marriage is linked to the woman's age at her first marriage; the older a woman is at the first marriage, the longer that marriage is likely to last.

- The percent of men divorced increased from 2 percent in 1950 to 8.2 percent in 1998.

- The divorce rate for married women increased from 8.8 per 1,000 women in 1940 to 20.9 per 1,000 women in 1990.

- The most remarriages (31.3 percent) of women in 1990 were 35 to 44 years old.

- 16 percent of women remarrying in 1990 were 45 to 64 years old, compared to 8 percent being 20 to 24 years old.

- 2.7 percent of remarriages in 1990 were women 65 years old and older, compared to 0.6 percent being younger than 20 years old.

- About one-third of remarrying men in 1990 were 35 to 44 years old, compared to about 20 percent being 30 to 34 years old.

- Another 24 percent of remarrying men in 1990 were 45 to 64 years old, compared to about 14 percent being 25 to 29 years old.

- 75 percent of divorced women remarry within 10 years.

Single: Gay without a Partner

Gays are increasingly an important part of our society. In a study by the US Census Bureau in 2004, 600,000 partners of the same sex are living together. [viii] The Los Angeles Times, reporting the results of a 1985 survey, stated that 10% of the national sample identified themselves as gay (Kirk, 1989).[ix]

In a study done by the US Census Bureau in 2003[x] it was found that same-sex unmarried-partner households comprised 0.6% of all households in both 2000 and 2003; 0.3% were male and 0.3% were female. Of this number 4.5 percent lived in mostly in large metropolitan areas.

- Male and female same-sex partners tended to be more educated than those who were either married or opposite-sex unmarried partners (25% and 26%, respectively, where both had a BA or more).

- 37.8% of female same-sex unmarried-partner households and 26.5% of male same-sex unmarried-partner households had children under 18 living with them as well.

In summary, same-sex unmarried-partner households looked very similar to married-couple households except they had slightly more education and were less likely to have children in the household.

I found relatively little information[xi] concerning the nature of dating and intimacy as it evolves over time in the relationships of gay (homosexual) men and women. Although older gay people experience the same bodily changes with aging and many of the same emotions as do older straight (heterosexual) people, they may also face unique challenges, such as the loss of a partner through HIV infection and a higher risk of social isolation. All of these stresses can be made worse when the healthy long-term partner is not even acknowledged as a legitimate guardian, caregiver, grieving partner, or beneficiary. Indeed, the stress that HIV infection places on a relationship can even drive some couples apart.

Fortunately, the evolution of the gay community has created a much stronger and more integrated community for older gay men and women.

The Kinsey Institute survey, reported by Bell and Weinberg in 1978, reported only 10 percent of gays in a long-term relationship. Gays who are "close-coupled," they report, don't abandon cruising; they do less cruising. The data was collected during the 1970's in gay bars, where close-coupled gay men were likely to be under-represented. Today the AIDS epidemic is undoubtedly increasing the number of gay men attempting to establish stable partnerships. [xii]

Single: Never Married

Statistics from the Commerce Department Census Bureau[xiii] has shown that the number of people marrying and/or staying married has steadily decreased over the last 30 years. The following chart shows the difference in the median age in which people married between 1994 and 2003. I think it is interesting to note that the difference in marriage age changed more in women between 1994 and 2003 than it did for men.[xiv] As a thought, if we figure out that every six years people are going to start marrying 2 years later by the year 2012 the average age will be 28 years. Gee, that was the age that my sister was writing me off as an old maid!

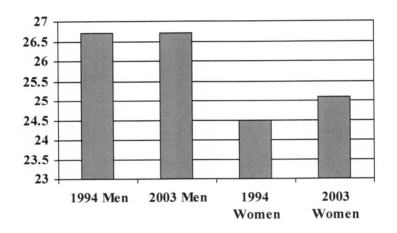

Comparison of Age Married 1994-2003

The number of unmarried persons rose from 28 to 34.7[xv] percent, while currently married adults declined from 72 to 61 percent.

Another bit of food for thought: Since 1970[xvi], the proportion of men and women who have never married has at least doubled and in some cases tripled for people between the ages of 25 and 44. Among persons 35 to 39 years old, the proportion of never married adults more than doubled from 5 to 13 percent for women and tripled from 7 to 19 percent for men, during this same period.

People are marrying later in age these days.

People are getting married later in life for a number of reasons:

- Contraception – around 1970 women started taking The Pill. This resulted in fewer pre-marital pregnancies and "shot-gun" weddings.

- Abortions became legal – again less need to "Have To" get married when a pregnancy occurred. Both women and men have more options now.

- Women started entering the workforce. Their pay has been steadily increasing which has meant they can afford to live on their own and not marry just to "get out of the house."

These facts gave men a freedom they had never known. They started getting involved in more activities they enjoyed and found less reason to get married.

Mindful Note

Although I made a concerned effort to write this book so it applied to any type of single, you may notice that much if it may apply to a single-never married. Please, take a second look, if you are widowed, divorced, or gay and see how the information may also apply to you.

Married Living With Spouse – The Dwindling Many

In the year 2001, only about 1 out of every 2 women was married and living with her spouse. This doesn't mean they never married, it just means that they weren't married when the survey was taken. But still, when you (or I) walk down the street on the average only 50% of the people we see are actually married. So, maybe when we sit alone on Saturday nights feeling lonely, we are focusing on the married people and not the single? when in reality only every other person in the U.S. is married. I don't know about you, but when I was single that would have made me feel better, realizing I wasn't alone in being alone.

Fewer people are marrying, having children or even staying with the person they marry.

1-in-10 People Never Marry[xvii]

I was pretty surprised when I saw that about 1 in 10 people **never** marry. I mean they never walk down that aisle and announce to the world that they're hitched. OK, even if you discount priests who can't marry and gays (who in most states) can't legally marry – still that is a lot: 1 in 10 people. I know when I was single and over 40 I thought I was one of so few. But, I guess not so much. The fact is the marriage rate in the U.S. dropped to 7.5 marriages per 1,000 population in 2003, the lowest rate in 40 years. [xviii]

And When We Do Marry?

What about those people who do marry? Well, it seems about half of the first marriages end in divorce, according to a report released today by the Commerce Department's Census Bureau. "Most adults have married only once," said Rose Kreider, co-author of Number, Timing and Duration of Marriages and Divorces: 1996. "In 1996, 54 percent of men and 60 percent of women married only once."

According to the same source, the average length of a first marriage is about eight years. Among those who had remarried, the median number of years before they married again was about three. The median duration of second marriages that ended in divorce was about seven years.

Some other interesting facts on divorce:

- In 1996, 8 percent of men and 10 percent of women were currently divorced, although 20 percent of men and 22 percent of women had been divorced at least once before.

- In 1996, about 13 percent of men and women had been married twice, while 3 percent of men and women had been married three or more times.

On a positive note, about 52 percent of currently married couples had reached at least their 15th anniversary in 1996, and 5 percent of them had reached at least their golden anniversary (50 years).

Numbers of Divorced Adults Increasing

Let's talk about divorce a little bit more, because I know a lot of you out there became single through divorce. Between 1970 and 1996, the number of divorced persons has more than quadrupled, from 4.3 million to 18.3 million. Quadrupled – that's four times over!!! It seems that wherever you look people are getting divorced. Family members: for example my sister. Rich people: Donald and Ivana Trump. Rock Stars: Tommi Lee and Pamela Anderson; Movie Actors: Demi Moore and Bruce Willis; Politicians: Rudy Giuliani and Donna Hanover. I wonder why it is that so many more people are getting divorced these days. Maybe it is because more women are active income earners (therefore not dependent on their husbands) According to the April 1998 Bureau of Labour Statistics, in 1966, only 35% of married women were active income earners, but by 1998, that number had doubled. More women also own their own business which takes up a lot of their time. In 1992 6.4 women-owned businesses made up 33 percent of all domestic firms and 40 percent of all retail and service firms. Women-owned businesses generated $1.6 trillion in revenues and employed 13.2 million people in 1992.

"High levels of divorce and postponement of first marriage are among the changes that have reshaped the living arrangements of children and adults since the 1970s," said Terry Lugaila, a Census Bureau analyst.

Mindful Note

From my married point of view, I don't think that just having your own money is a reason to get divorced. That may just be a tool, maybe a tool that makes divorce easier when things aren't going well in your marriage, you'll have money to live on by yourself. I wasn't able to find any reliable comparison between the number of households that ended in divorce where there were two incomes and the numbers that ended in divorce that had only one income.

Between You and Your Parents

Things have changed between the time since our parents were married and now. It seems like everything our parents did, they did younger or not at all. Maybe after looking at some of the following facts we will realize why our parents are pushing us to get married.

- The number of unmarried-couple households (couples of opposite sexes) grew from 523,000 in 1970 to 4 million in 1996.

- In 1950 the divorce rate was 2.2 percent, in 2000 that rate increased to 4.1 percent.

- Between 1970 and 1996, the number of women living alone doubled from 7.3 million to 14.6 million, while the number of men living alone tripled, from 3.5 million to 10.3 million.

More Single-Person Households Every Day[xix]

So, what are we doing? We are living alone. In fact, in 1994 12 percent of all adults lived alone. By 2000, those numbers increased to one-quarter of all homes being occupied by single person. While women accounted for the larger share of persons living alone in 1994 (6 of 10), the number of men living alone increased at a faster pace. It is predicted by 2030 nearly three out of 10 working households (29.2 percent) will consist of single persons living alone. I tend to think that this number wouldn't be increasing if it wasn't for the fact that people are *enjoying* living by themselves.

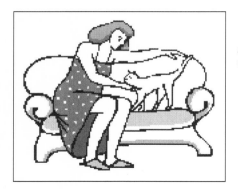

An increasing number of people are living alone – and loving it!

Between Single and Married: Cohabitation

Co-habitation is a time where you are not really single, but not really married (though you may live like a married couple). When I was in my 20's and 30's I didn't think that there was any point in being married, unless I was going to have a child. Therefore, since I didn't have any children, I lived with two different men during two special stretches of times. I was quite contented with my living situations, thank you very much. I felt that I had my freedom as a single person, while still having someone to come home to at night. We had what might be called a temporary commitment to one another, we bought furniture together, and we planned vacations. We felt bonded; at least I did (remember that cheating boyfriend). In my 40's, I decided I wanted to be married because something inside me needed more of a commitment. I wanted to make plans 10 years in advance; the length of commitment that I felt was not present in my co-habitation situation. I wanted to see myself partnered with a person as I grew older. I wanted to see us really work out our differences, and to grow from our differences. Therefore, I married and I must say I feel we have worked out some major differences that I do not think we would have worked out if we weren't married. So, I can see the benefits of both being married and cohabitating.

I wasn't alone in my cohabitation situations. Recently the National Center for Disease Control and Prevention[xx] surveyed 11,000 women[1] on marriage and divorce. More than a third of U.S. women had lived with a boyfriend or partner before marrying him. While 70% of those who had lived together for at least five years did get married, 40% had divorced within 10 years. (For couples who had not lived together prior to marrying, 31% broke up within ten years.)

That Ticking Clock[xxi]

What about children? Do we have to get married to have children? Can we give birth after we reach the age of 40? Among all women ages 40 to 44, those who were childless increased from 10 percent in 1976 to 19 percent in 1998. So, we are not only delaying having a child a bit, but we're also thinking about having one without a partner.

Deciding when to have a child can be determined by your ticking clock rather than your marital status.

If you decide to have a child on your own, you won't be alone there either. The number of single mothers increased between 1970 and 2000, from 3 million to 10 million; over the same time frame, the number of single fathers increased also, from 393,000 to 2 million. Of the nation's single women, 33% had given birth to at least one child prior to a 2002 survey[xxii] by the Commerce Department's Census Bureau.

---

[1] While researching this book, I found that most of the studies done by the National Center for Disease Control and Prevention were on women.

"The delay in first marriages and rise in divorce among adults are two of the major factors contributing to the growing proportion of children in one-parent living situations," said Arlene Saluter[xxiii], the report's author. Between 1970 and 1994, the proportion of children living with two parents (biological, step, or adoptive) declined from 85 to 69 percent. "Children are considerably more likely to be living with only one parent today than in 1970," Ms. Saluter said. "In 1994, 27 percent of children under 18 lived with one parent, up from 12 percent in 1970. The majority--88 percent--of these children lived with their mothers, but an increasing proportion lived with their fathers (9 percent in 1970 vs. 12 percent in 1994)."

Mindful Note

If you are gay and looking to adopt, check out this website that provides some how to hints: http://www.ehow.com/how_16930_adopt-child-gay/lesbian.html

Additional Facts About Being Single

There are 82 million unmarried adults in the United States. Singles constitute more than 40% of the adult population in the nation. In many major metropolitan areas, singles comprise the majority of the adult population. The Census Bureau estimates that about 10% of adults will never marry. So, what are all the single people up to?

Where Are Those Single Folks Living

Single people have decided to spend more time living with their parents or another person. In fact...

- Singles in Massachusetts are getting married the latest, men wait until age 29 and women age 27.
- Single adults living alone comprise about 25% of the nation's households.
- Another 13 million single adults are living with unmarried relatives.
- Nearly 6% of the nation's households are composed of two unrelated adults living together, with 68% of these households containing partners of the opposite sex.
- Singles tend to be renters rather than home owners.
  - ➢ Single people live in only 31% of the nation's 65 million owner-occupied units.
  - ➢ Single people live in 62% of the nation's 34 million rental units.

States Where Singles are Marrying Latest

Do you want to be around likeminded single people? Go to Massachusetts or Washington D.C. Massachusetts is the state where singles are waiting until they are older to get married. Here is the top ten list.[xxiv]

1	Massachusetts
2	New York
3	Connecticut
4	New Jersey
5	Vermont
6	Hawaii
7	Rhode Island
8	Pennsylvania
9	New Hampshire
10	California

Washington D.C. (which I'm not sure we can count as a state) singles were getting married the latest (30.1 for men, 29.9 for women).

Older Adults

According to a study done by the American Association of Retired Persons only 36 percent of older women live with their spouses, compared to over 60 percent of older men. 35 percent of older women live alone, compared with 14 percent of older men. Among those age 85 and over, 53% of women live alone, compared with 25% of men.[xxv]

People with Disabilities

According to the Disability Statistics Rehabilitation Research and Training Center, of the 32 million adults in the United States who have disabilities, some 13 million (40%) are unmarried. [xxvi]

Premarital Sex

I thought that this bit of information would tickle your fancy:[xxvii]

- Of those born between 1933 and 1942: 22% of men and 54% of women were virgins, compared to those born between 1963 and 1974 where 16% of men and 20% of women were virgins.

It's the Law!!

Discrimination Against Single People

Single individuals, unmarried couples, and non-marital families experience a wide variety of discrimination-related problems. Some of these problems include:

- Criminal laws that impose penalties for consenting sex in private
- Fewer benefits than for married employees
- Programs that exclude unmarried heterosexual couples
- Being refused housing by some landlords, especially those landlords who have bias against singles
- Higher insurance rates
- No joint insurance policy for domestic partners
- Higher taxes than a married couple (though these laws are continually changing)
- Being denied child custody or having visitation restrictions if living with a domestic partner

Do Your State's Civil Rights Laws Include Marital Status?[xxviii]

Some states have laws that bar discrimination against singles. Do you live in one of them? Appendix A contains a table that lists whether you state has one of the following laws against discrimination.

- Employment
- Housing
- Insurance
- Credit

Mindful Note

Check out Appendix A to see if you are one of the fortunate singles who is protected by your state.

Now That You Know

I tried to present in this chapter some facts that put unpartnered folks on the road to reality about being single. Even though we walk down the street and (think we) see mostly married people, the fact is – only about half of the people we meet are not married.

It's time to look at the real reasons YOU want to marry. Is it to have a child? Well, you can see that a high percentage of people are having children on their own, even men and gays are adopting at a higher frequency. Therefore, decide to have a child when you know have the love and time to invest. Is it for companionship? If you expect that your partner will always be there at your beck and call – take another look: More people are working more hours. More couples have to "schedule" their time together because of their busy schedules. In this day and age, married life does not mean sharing every (or even many) spare minute(s) together. Therefore, marry someone with whom you know you would want to share every single day of your life.

Sharing, caring and lowered expectations *can* lead to a lifetime of marital bliss. Humans, as part of the animal species, want to hook up with another similar being. We, by nature, don't want to be alone. So, once we set our sights on reality and mindfully decide what we really want, then that is the time to get married or stay single (at least for a period of time).

Now that you know the fact of the matter: You are not alone being alone, then maybe it's time to move on and take care of those things you've been delaying, like buying a new car or fixing up your home. Chapter 2 will show you how to get on with your life. It even offers suggestions on what to do so that you don't get hoodwinked.

End Note

As with all surveys, the data contained in the chapter is subject to sampling and other sources of error.

Chapter 2 Making Large Purchases with Confidence

"If you have no confidence in self, you are twice defeated in the race of life. With confidence, you have won even before you have started."

Marcus Tullius Cicero
(Ancient Roman Lawyer, Writer, Scholar, Orator and Statesman, 106-43 BC)

When you are single you may feel held back because a part of you doesn't want to make any large long term investments. You may think ... "well, I'll do that when I get a permanent partner". Yet again, you may feel afraid you will be taken advantage of, if you take on a major task or make a large purchase; and still another part of you may feel you just can't do it because you don't have the skills or knowledge.

The first chapter of this book let you know that there are many other singles out there just like you who want to move on and become settled in their present lifestyle. Do you wonder if it is time you bought a house, or a new car?

Are you hesitant about making a large purchase? Afraid the sales person will not give you as good a deal because you don't have a partner standing beside you? Many un-partnered people feel this way. Armed with the knowledge of the process of making large purchases you can feel empowered. This chapter will provide that knowledge. It covers a myriad of financial topics and, answers some of the following questions:

- How do I get the best deal when buying a car?

- How do I get a mortgage to buy a home?

- How do I get credit? How do I know I'm not getting discriminated against when I do?

- What are the steps to get a home improvement project done right?

- How do I go about investing my money?

- Where do I go for help when all this goes wrong?

After you read this chapter you will feel more confident when you make large purchases. You will know what to expect when you buy something and what to do if something goes wrong (no, not just complain to your best friend!!)

Buying a Car

Nothing is worse than either going in to buy a car or having a car repair done, and the service person looks at you as though you're an idiot when you ask any questions. This section will let you know the right questions to ask when buying a car or having that new car (or your current car) repaired.

Be certain that all the t's are crossed and the i's are dotted before making that deal.

Making the Deal

After buying a home, buying a car is your next major purchase. Buying a car as a single person can be intimidating, especially if you are an unattached woman. When I went to buy a car for myself, even as a married woman, all they wanted to do was to talk my husband – who was more than happy to discuss the details, even though I was more knowledgeable about the type of car I wanted. I was just left there twiddling my thumbs, until I forced my way into the conversation and described what I wanted. At that point I was paid more attention. I learned that being assertive, having the proper information and asking the right questions kept the salespersons' attention and got me the best deal.

- Remember: buying a car is a negotiated transaction. Actually it's several distinct negotiated transactions, including:
  - ➢ Buying a car;
  - ➢ Selling your trade-in;
  - ➢ Arranging for financing; and
  - ➢ Potentially buying other products and services such as vehicle protection packages, extended service contracts, etc.
- Know how much your trade-in is worth by checking the Kelly Blue Book (www.kbb.com/) or the National Auto Dealers Association (NADA) Used Car Pricing Guide (www.nadaguides.com/) available at your bank or local library.
- Know how much you can afford to spend before you go shopping and compare financing terms between the dealers' bank and credit unions.

- Take a thorough test drive. Operate the vehicle as you would in normal use.

- Always have used vehicles thoroughly inspected by an independent mechanic of your choice prior to agreeing to purchase the vehicle.

- Get all promises in writing. Read and understand every document you sign. *Don't sign anything with blank spaces before it.* Your signature binds you contractually to make all payments.

- Check out the history of used vehicles by requesting the name and address of the prior owner from the dealer. Dealers are required to provide it to you if you are a prospective purchaser.

- Remember that there is no three-day cooling-off period or cancellation rights when purchasing a new or used vehicle. Once you sign the contract, you own the car and are obligated to make all payments.

What to do if You Have a Problem Buying a Car

To report problems with an auto service provider, or dealer, contact your local and state consumer protection agencies, including the state insurance commissioner and state attorney general. Also, contact law schools in your area and ask if they have dispute resolution programs.

Mindful Note

Some of the agencies that I have suggested are listed on page 47 of this book, others (like the State Attorney General) are specific to your state and you can find them either in your phone book or on the internet.

Auto Repair

When your car is making a funny noise, you can feel at the mechanic's mercy when you bring it in for a repair. I mean I'm not a mechanic and wouldn't know if that screech I hear is the engine falling apart, or a loose nut on the transmission. My friend Eva surely would have gotten hoodwinked if she hadn't gotten a second opinion. Let me tell you what she said.

There was one time I can think of when I brought my car in and the mechanic told me I needed a new transmission that would cost hundreds of dollars. I said I wanted to get another quote and they said I didn't need one. I do not know if I was told I needed a new transmission because I was a woman or that was just how they operated. I did end up getting a second option and I never needed a new transmission for the car and I have since owned it for five more years.

Now, Eva was smart to get that second opinion, even though the first mechanic suggested she shouldn't (I wonder why???). If Eva did not have the confidence to go to another mechanic she would have been out of a few hundred dollars.

Many people, like Karyn who has been divorced for a number of years, just hate dealing with the mechanics of machinery, so she is grateful that she has a mechanic she can trust. She says...

Mechanical things, I hate mechanical things: heavy lifting; diagnosing car problems.

Before you have repairs done:

- Ask family and friends for recommendations of any good mechanics or car repair shops.

- Check out the repair shop with your local Better Business Bureau.

- Get a second opinion.

- Before you have the work done, ask about any warranties covering the repair and get those warranties in writing.

Keep yourself covered:

- Ask for damaged parts to be saved.

- Ask for the written estimate for which you are entitled, on repairs over $100.00 if you deal face-to-face.

- Be sure to tell the mechanic that your permission is required if repairs are more than 10 percent over the authorized estimate.

Buying a Home

It can be quite scary trying to obtain a mortgage if you do not know some preliminary facts. Karyn tells how she delayed buying a home:

I'm not waiting until I get married to make major purchases, but it did take me years before I decided to buy a house. At one time I was looking at who my partner would be first. I'm sure I would handle my finances differently if I were married. I'd have another person to be concerned with. This way, I don't and I really like that.

If, like Karyn, you are ready to buy a home, it is always good to begin this endeavor with the best information. This section provides the steps you need to take to obtain a mortgage. It includes the following information:

- Finding the best mortgage
- Obtaining Home Equity Credit Lines

- Identifying Mortgage discrimination

Five Steps to Finding the Best Mortgage

Shopping around for a home loan or mortgage will lead you to the best financing deal. A mortgage—whether it's to buy a home, refinance it, or a get a home equity loan -- is a product, just like a car, so the price and terms may be negotiable. You'll want to compare all the costs involved in obtaining a mortgage. Shopping, comparing, and negotiating may save you thousands of dollars. The following five steps should get you started in obtaining the best mortgage possible.

1. Decide how much you can afford to spend.

2. Know the type of mortgage you want.

3. Obtain mortgage information from several lenders.

4. Compare all costs involved in each loan offer.

5. Negotiate for the best mortgage.

1. Decide How Much You Can Afford to Spend

Your first step when deciding to buy a home is to know how much you can afford. This cost does not only include your monthly payment but all other fees involved in obtaining the loan.

- **Monthly Payment:**   Many sites on the internet, such as http://www.mortgage101.com provide calculators that will determine how much mortgage you can afford to pay. All you do is enter information such as your salary and living expenses and you will receive an estimate of the monthly home payment that you can afford. This estimate includes:

  - ➢ Principal and Interest

  - ➢ Real Estate Taxes

  - ➢ Hazard Insurance

  - ➢ Private Mortgage Insurance

  It is also a good idea at this time to obtain a credit report. A consumer credit report[xxix] is a factual record of your payment history. Its main purpose is to help a lender quickly and objectively decide whether to grant you credit. Examples of credit include car loans, credit cards and home mortgages. You may obtain a free credit report once a year; check the internet, or your local library for details.

- **Up Front Money:** Review your savings account and see how much money you can pay for a down payment, up front fees, points, etc.

➢ **Down Payment:**[xxx] Some lenders require 20 percent of the home's purchase price as a down payment. However, many lenders now offer loans that require less than 20 percent down—sometimes as little as 5 percent on conventional loans. When government-assisted programs such as FHA (Federal Housing Administration), VA (Veterans Administration), or Rural Development Services are available, the down payment requirements may be substantially smaller.

➢ **Points**: Fees paid to the lender for the loan. One point equals 1 percent of the loan amount. Points are usually paid in cash at closing. In some cases, the money needed to pay points can be borrowed, but doing so will increase the loan amount and the total costs.

➢ **Fees**: A home loan often involves many fees, such as loan origination or underwriting fees, transaction fees, settlement, and closing costs. Some fees are paid when you apply for a loan (such as application and appraisal fees), and others are paid at closing. In some cases, you can borrow the money needed to pay these fees, but doing so will increase your loan amount and total costs. "No cost" loans are sometimes available, but they usually involve higher rates.

➢ Private Mortgage Insurance (PMI): Lenders usually require the home buyer to purchase a (PMI) to protect the lender in case the home buyer fails to pay.

2. Know the Type of Mortgage You Want

Decide on what type of mortgage you want, depending on your current and future financial ability.

- **Adjustable Rate Mortgages (ARMS):** Start at a low rate which adjusts following a set schedule. If you are training in a career that pays more money after training is completed, you might choose a lower payment to get started in your home, expecting to have the house payment increase in the future.[xxxi]

- **Balloon Mortgages:** Have low monthly payments, but require re-financing or pay off at the end of the initial term, sometime three years. If you will be moving and selling at the same time your balloon mortgage is due, this might be an option for you.

- **THDA Mortgages:** Fixed rate mortgage designed for families of low or moderate incomes. THDA mortgages are offered at lower-than-market interest rates through local lenders.

- **Fixed Rate Mortgages:** The most common type of mortgage. Fixed rate mortgages lock into today's rates. You pay the same mortgage amount for the length of your loan.

- **Jumbo Loan:** A loan which is larger (more than $240,000 as of 1/1/99) than the limits set by the Federal National Mortgage Association and the Federal Home Loan Mortgage Corporation. Because jumbo loans cannot be funded by these two agencies, they usually carry a higher interest rate.

Mindful Note

Even though a Reverse Mortgage is not your typical type of mortgage, I thought I would include a little bit of information about it here, for those who are curious as to what it is. Most important: do not confuse it with a regular type of mortgage. A Reverse Mortgage allows older homeowners (over 62) to convert part of the equity in their homes into cash without having to sell their homes or take on additional monthly bills. In a "regular" mortgage, you make monthly payments to the lender. But in a "reverse" mortgage, you receive money from the lender and generally don't have to pay it back for as long as you live in your home. Instead, the loan must be repaid when you die, sell your home, or no longer live there as your principal residence.[xxii]

3. Obtain Mortgage Information from Several Lenders

Your local newspaper, phone book and the Internet are good places to start shopping for mortgage lenders. Home loans are available from several types of lenders -- commercial banks, mortgage companies, and credit unions are examples. Lenders may quote you different prices, so you should contact several lenders to make sure you are getting the best price.

Since you now know how much of a mortgage you can afford, this is the time to research and see what types of mortgages are available for you. Being aware of the amount of the monthly payment or the interest rate is *not* enough information to know. Ask for the details about the loan so that in the next step you can compare all your options.

- Find out from each lender a list of its current mortgage interest rates and whether the rates being quoted are the lowest for that day or week.

- Discover whether the interest rate is fixed or adjustable. A fixed rate is one that will remain throughout the life of the loan; an adjustable rate (ARM) fluctuates with the market. The initial interest rate of an ARM will usually be lower than that of most fixed rate loans. Initial rates for ARMs can be as much as three percentage points lower than a 30 year fixed rate mortgage. Then, as the country's economy and national interest rates fluctuate, your ARM's interest rate will fluctuate with it. Keep in mind that when interest rates for adjustable-rate loans go up, generally so does the monthly payment.

- Learn as much information as possible about the loan's annual percentage rate (APR). The APR takes into account not only the interest rate but also points, fees, and certain other credit charges that you may be required to pay, expressed as a yearly rate.

- Discover if you can get a better deal by paying points. When you pay points you may get a lower interest rate, but paying thousands more dollars in up front costs. Check your local newspaper for information about rates and points currently being offered. Try to get points quoted to you as a dollar amount – rather than just as the number of points – so that you will actually know how much you will have to pay.

Mindful Note

Check out the sections in this book on pages 26 and 27 about how to recognize shady lenders and what to be aware of when taking out a loan.

4. Compare All Costs Involved in Each Loan Offer

Now, take the information you just learned in Step 2 and compare it. Use the worksheet[xxxiii] presented in Appendix B to do this task. The worksheet asks you to enter the information about *two* lenders. Make copies of the worksheet if you want to compare more than two lenders. This worksheet is quite complete in that you can use it not only to compare the basic information about each lender – such as the type of mortgage and length of loan, but also other details such as mortgage fees, insurance and possible penalties. Therefore you can choose the best mortgage possible based on all the facts.

Mindful Note

Don't worry if you can't fill in all the fields on the worksheet for each lender, just complete as much information as you can, and compare from there.

5. Negotiate for the Best Mortgage

Once you know what each lender has to offer, compare the costs and terms you discovered in the previous step then negotiate with your lender of choice for the best deal. This is also the time to negotiate with the seller of your dream house for the best possible price. Here are some ways you can negotiate for the best price for your home:

- **Assume an existing mortgage:** Take over the existing mortgage on a house, rather than getting a new one. This is beneficial if, for example, the existing mortgage has a lower interest rate. You can also avoid some of the administrative costs of taking out a new loan.

- **Seller financing:** "Seller financing" means that you can pay the seller directly over a period of time, rather than borrow money and pay at once.

- **Play with the points, play with the time:** Ask for a reduction in the number of points or length of the mortgage.

Remember, mortgage lenders must compete for your business. That means they will negotiate. Don't assume that their published interest rates are final. Collect information on available interest rates and mortgage features from lenders in your area. Decide which features meet your needs. Be prepared to ask for better terms -- a reduction of at least a quarter percent of the published interest rate is reasonable. You will be in a stronger negotiating position if your credit history is good.

Mindful Note

Now that you have all the information about mortgages and the best rates, before you go house shopping this may be the time to look into getting a pre-approved mortgage. A pre-approved mortgage qualifies you for a mortgage before you start shopping for a home. You know exactly how much you can spend and are free to make a "firm" offer when you find the right home. Remember, just because you get a pre-approved mortgage from a lender, you are not required to take out your mortgage with them, though you will be locked into an interest rate with them if you do.

Home Equity Credit Lines

You've lived in your home for a number of years and have built up equity (in other words your house is worth more than you owe on the mortgage). At this point you may want to look into getting a home equity credit line to fix up your home or even buy a car. Using a credit line to borrow against the equity in your home has become a popular source of consumer credit. And lenders are offering these home equity credit lines in a variety of ways.

You will find most loans come with variable interest rates, some come with attractive low introductory rates, and a few come with fixed rates. You also may find most loans have large one-time upfront fees, others have closing costs, and some have continuing costs, such as annual fees. You can find loans with large balloon payments at the end of the loan, and others with no balloons but with higher monthly payments.

With a Home Equity Line, you can take money out of your home, while you still live in it.

Unfortunately, if you agree to a loan that's based on the equity you have in your home; you may be putting your most valuable asset at risk. Homeowners-particularly elderly, minority and those with low incomes or poor credit-should be careful when borrowing money based on their home equity. Why? Certain abusive or exploitative lenders target these borrowers, who unwittingly may be putting their homes on the line.

What to Look Out for When Getting a Loan

Abusive lending practices range from equity stripping and loan flipping to hiding loan terms and packing a loan with extra charges. The Federal Trade Commission urges you to be aware of these loan practices to avoid losing your home.

Look out for: A lender that encourages you to "pad" your income on your application form to get the loan approved.

Reason: As soon as you cannot meet your payments, the lender forecloses-on your home; stripping you of the equity you have spent years building.

Look out for: A lender who provides you a mortgage where the payments are extremely low.

Reason: The payments may be lower because the lender is offering a loan on which you repay only the interest each month. At the end of the loan term, the principal-that is, the entire amount that you borrowed-is due in one lump sum called a balloon payment. If you can't make the balloon payment or refinance, you face foreclosure and the loss of your home.

Look out for: A contractor who wants to arrange financing, and at some time during the project you are asked to sign a lot of papers. The papers may be blank or the lender may rush you to sign before you have time to read what you've been given.

Reason: The interest rate, points and fees may be very high. To make matters worse, the work on your home is not done right or hasn't been completed, and the contractor, who may have been paid by the lender, has little interest in completing the work to your satisfaction.

Look out for: At closing, the lender gives you papers to sign that include charges for credit insurance or other "benefits" that you did not ask for and do not want.

Reason: If you agree to buy the insurance, you really are paying extra for the loan by buying a product you may not want or need.

Look out for: If you are having trouble paying your mortgage and the lender has threatened to foreclose and take your home, another "lender" may contact you with an offer to help you find new financing. They may ask you to deed your property to them, claiming that it's a temporary measure to prevent foreclosure.

Reason: The promised refinancing that would let you save your home never comes through. Once the lender has the deed to your property, they start to treat it as their own. They may borrow against it (for their benefit, not yours) or even sell it to someone else.

Identifying Mortgage Discrimination

The Equal Credit Opportunity Act (ECOA) and the Fair Housing Act (FHA) protect you against discrimination when you apply for a mortgage to purchase, refinance, or make home improvements.

Lenders must:

- Consider reliable public assistance income in the same way as other income.

- Consider reliable income from part-time employment, Social Security, pensions, and annuities.

- Consider reliable alimony, child support, or separate maintenance payments, if you choose to provide this information. A lender may ask you for proof that this income is received consistently.

- If a co-signer is needed, accept someone other than your spouse. If you own the property with your spouse, he or she may be asked to sign documents allowing you to mortgage the property.

Lenders cannot:

- Discourage you from applying for a mortgage or reject your application because of your race, national origin, religion, sex, marital status, age, or because you receive public assistance income.

- Consider your race, national origin, or sex, although you will be asked to voluntarily disclose this information to help federal agencies enforce anti-discrimination laws. A creditor may consider your immigration status and whether you have the right to remain in the country long enough to repay the debt.

- Impose different terms or conditions, such as a higher interest rate or larger down payment, on a loan based on your race, sex, or other prohibited factors.

- Consider the racial composition of the neighborhood where you want to live. This also applies when the property is being appraised.

- Ask about your plans for having a family. Questions about expenses related to your dependents are permitted.

- Refuse to provide a loan or set different terms or conditions for the loan purchase based on discriminatory factors.

- Require a co-signer if you meet the lender's standards.

If You Feel You Have Been Discriminated Against

You've taken all (or at least most) of the steps to apply for a loan, you've been sure to read what to look out for with a lender, but still you are having problems. In fact, you think you have been discriminated against. What do you do now? Here are some suggestions if you feel you have been discriminated against when applying for a mortgage:

- Complain to the lender. Sometimes you can persuade the lender to reconsider your application.

- Check with your state Attorney General's office to see if the creditor violated state laws. Many states have their own equal credit opportunity laws.

- Contact a local private fair housing group and report violations to the appropriate government agency. If your mortgage application is denied, the lender must give you the name and address of the agency to contact.

- Consider suing the lender in federal district court. If you win, you can recover your actual damages and be awarded punitive damages if the court finds that the lender's conduct was willful. You also may recover reasonable lawyers' fees and court costs. You also might consider joining with others to file a class action suit.

- A number of federal agencies share enforcement responsibility for the ECOA and the Federal Housing Administration (FHA). Determining which agency to contact depends, in part, on the type of financial institution you dealt with.

Take action if you have been discriminated against.

For ECOA violations involving mortgage and consumer finance companies:

Federal Trade Commission
Consumer Response Center
Washington, DC 20580
202-326-2222; TDD: 1-866-653-4261

While the FTC generally does not intervene in individual disputes, the information you provide may indicate a pattern of violations requiring action by the Commission. The FTC also can provide you with a copy of *Best Sellers*, a complete list of FTC consumer and business publications. You can visit the FTC at www.ftc.gov on the internet.

For violations of the FHA:

Office of Fair Housing and Equal Opportunity
US Department of Housing and Urban
Development (HUD), Room 5204
Washington, DC 20410-2000

For More Information on Home Lending Issues

For more information on home lending issues, visit www.consumer.gov, write to the Consumer Information Center, Pueblo, CO 81009 or visit the Center's Web site (http://www.pueblo.gsa.gov/). The following brochures are available from their web site:

- A Consumer's Guide to Mortgage Refinancing
- Buying Your Home: Settlement Costs and Helpful Information

- Consumer Handbook on Adjustable Rate Mortgages
- Guide to Single Family Home Mortgage Insurance
- Home Buyer's Vocabulary
- Home Mortgages: Understanding the Process and Your Rights to Fair Lending
- How to Buy a Home with a Low Down Payment
- How to Dispute Credit Report Errors
- The HUD Home Buying Guide
- When Your Home Is on the Line

Eight Steps to Getting a Home Improvement Job Done Right

You've got the mortgage and you own what you thought was your dream house. Then you saw you wanted a larger kitchen or a new bath, so you got a home equity loan. Now, it's time to make sure this new bath is done right. This section will provide the eight steps necessary for getting your home improvement job done right.

Whether you're planning to put down new floors or fix a hole in the wall, finding a competent and reliable contractor is the first step to a successful and satisfying home improvement project. Many people, like Mary, feel a bit intimidated when they have to get a home repair completed:

Taking care of a house would be much easier if I had a partner. I do not like to deal with handymen and car repair people because I feel I am being taken advantaged of.

Karyn has learned from experience that she doesn't need a partner to get tasks done around her home:

I've been out here for a long time, so I have friends that will help me; I do decorating myself or get help from my family/friends. I guess I feel pretty self sufficient and I get help from folks that are available from my pool of friends or family.

It's important to be cautious when you hire someone to work in your home. You should not only be concerned with getting a job done right, but also for protecting your other valuables. We all can't be like Karyn and have friends or family provide us referrals to quality workers. Sometimes we have to look in a newspaper or the Yellow Pages.

Mindful Note

Remember, just because you see an advertisement in a reputable place, that ad doesn't indicate the quality of work or character of the professional.

Who do you call when your house has problems?

Being hoodwinked by a contractor professional is one of a single person's (heck even a married person's) worst fears. But, how do you choose and work with a contractor when you want to put in a new bathroom shower stall or perform any other home improvement? Take the following steps to improve your chances of getting the job done right.

1. Choose the right type of contract professional.

2. Interview the contractor.

3. Get and check references.

4. Understand your payment options.

5. Obtain a written contract.

6. Keep records throughout the project.

7. Complete a checklist to complete the job.

8. If you have a problem – let it be known!!

1. Choose the Right Type of Contract Professional

Depending on the size and complexity of your project, you may choose to work with one or more of these specialized contract professionals:

- **General Contractors** manage all aspects of your project, including hiring and supervising subcontractors, getting building permits, and scheduling inspections. They also work with architects and designers.

- **Specialty Contractors** have specific areas of expertise, for example they may just install cabinets or bathroom fixtures.

- **Architects** design homes, additions, and major renovations. If your project includes structural changes, you may want to hire an architect who specializes in home remodeling.

- **Designers** have expertise in specific areas of the home, such as kitchens and baths. They help you decide how your room should look, such as getting the best look by coordinating the colors in the walls, sofa and rug.

- **Design/Build Contractors** provide one-stop service. They see your project through from start to finish. Some firms have architects on staff; others use certified designers.

2. Interview the Contractor

Interview each person you're considering to hire. Find out what work they have done previously and check their references: Who have they worked with? What kind of job have they done? Find out about this person whom you are going to not only welcome into your home – but also allow to make changes you may have to live with the rest of your life. Here are some questions to ask.

- How long have you been in business? Look for a well-established company and check it out with consumer protection officials.

- Are you licensed and registered with the state?[xxxiv] While most states license electrical and plumbing contractors, only 36 states have some type of licensing and registration statutes affecting contractors, remodelers, and/or specialty contractors. The licensing can range from simple registration to a detailed qualification process.

- How many similar projects has the contractor completed in the last year? Ask for a list. Use this list to determine how familiar the contractor is with your type of project.

- Will your project require a permit? Most states and localities require permits for building projects, even for simple jobs like decks. Be suspicious if the contractor asks you to get the permit(s). It could mean that the contractor is not licensed or registered, as required by your state or locality.

- Will you be using subcontractors on this project? If yes, ask to meet them, and make sure they have current insurance coverage and licenses, if required. Also ask them if this contractor paid them on time.

- What types of insurance do they carry? Contractors should have personal liability, worker's compensation, and property damage coverage. Ask for copies of insurance certificates, and make sure they're current. Avoid doing business with contractors who don't carry the appropriate insurance. Otherwise, you'll be held liable for any injuries and damages that occur during the project.

Be sure to interview your contractor and check their references before hiring them.

3. Get and Check References

The contractor should be able to give you the names, addresses, and phone numbers of at least three clients who have had projects done that were similar to yours. Ask each how long ago the project was completed and if you can see it. Also, especially if this is a large project, tell the contractor that you'd like to visit jobs in progress. Talk with some of the contractor's former customers. They can help you decide if a particular contractor is right for you. You may want to ask the previous customer:

- Can I visit your home to see the completed job?

- Were you satisfied with the project? Was it completed on time?

- Did the contractor keep you informed about the status of the project, and were there any problems along the way?

- Were there unexpected costs? If so, what were they?

- Did workers show up on time? Did they clean up after finishing the job?

- Would you use the contractor again?

4. Understand Your Payment Options

You have several payment options for most home improvement and maintenance and repair projects. For example, you can get your own loan or ask the contractor to arrange financing for larger projects. For smaller projects, you may want to pay by check or credit card. Avoid paying cash. Whatever option you choose, be sure you have a reasonable payment schedule and a fair interest rate. Try to limit your down payment. Some state laws limit the amount of money a contractor can request as a down payment, if you have concerns. Contact your state or local consumer agency to find out what the law is in your area. Here are some additional tips:

- Try to make payments during the project contingent upon completion of a defined amount of work. This way, if the work is not proceeding according to schedule, the payment also is delayed.

- Don't make the final payment or sign an affidavit of final release until you are satisfied with the work and know that the subcontractors and suppliers have been paid.

- Some state or local laws limit the amount by which the final bill can exceed the estimate, unless you have approved the increase. Check with your local Consumer Protection Agency.

- If you have a problem with merchandise or services that you charged to a credit card and have made a good faith effort to work out the problem with the seller, you have the right to withhold from the card issuer payment for the merchandise or services. You can withhold payment up to the amount of credit outstanding for the purchase, plus any finance or related charges.

Mindful Note

Refer to page 25 if you have chosen to take a home equity line to finance this project.

5. Obtain a Written Contract[xxxv]

Contract requirements vary by state. Even if your state does not require a written agreement, ask for one. A contract spells out the who, what, where, when and cost of your project. The agreement should be clear, concise and complete. Before you sign a contract, make sure it contains:

- The contractor's name, address, phone, and license number, if required.

- The payment schedule for the contractor, subcontractors and suppliers.

- An estimated start and completion date.

- The contractor's obligation to obtain all necessary permits.

- How change orders will be handled. A change order — common on most remodeling jobs — is a written authorization to the contractor to make a change or addition to the work described in the original contract. It could affect the project's cost and schedule. Remodelers often require payment for change orders before work begins.

- A detailed list of all materials including color, model, size, brand name, and product.

- Warranties covering materials and workmanship. The names and addresses of the parties honoring the warranties — contractor, distributor or manufacturer — must be identified. The length of the warranty period and any limitations also should be spelled out.

- An exact description of the work. For example, is site clean-up and trash hauling included in the price? Ask for a "broom clause." It makes the contractor responsible for all clean-up work, including spills and stains.

- Oral promises also should be added to the written contract.

- A written statement of your right to cancel the contract within three business days if you signed it in your home or at a location other than the seller's permanent place of business. During the sales transaction, the salesperson (contractor) must give you two copies of a cancellation form (one to keep and one to send back to the company) and a copy of your contract or receipt. The contract or receipt must be dated, show the name and address of the seller, and explain your right to cancel.

- Signature of both parties

Get a written contract before making any major deal.

6. Keep Records Throughout the Project

Keep all paperwork related to your project in one place. This includes copies of the contract, service agreements, contracts, change orders and correspondence with your contractor. Keep a log or journal of all phone calls, conversations and activities. You also might want to take photographs as the job progresses. These records are especially important if you have problems with your project — during or after construction.

The paperwork you hoard today may save you a lot of headaches tomorrow.

7. Complete a Checklist to Complete the Job

Before you sign off and make the final payment, use the following checklist to make sure the job is complete.

- All work meets the standards spelled out in the contract.
- You have written warranties for materials and workmanship.
- You have proof that all subcontractors and suppliers have been paid.
- The job site has been cleaned up and cleared of excess materials, tools and equipment.
- You have inspected and approved the completed work.

8. If You Have a Problem with a Home Improvement Project

If you have a problem with your home improvement project, first try to resolve it with the contractor. Many disputes can be resolved at this level. Follow-up any phone conversations with a letter you send by certified mail. Request a return receipt which is your proof that the contractor received your letter. Keep a copy for your files.

If you can't get satisfaction with the contractor, consider contacting one of the following organizations for further information and help:

- State and local consumer protection offices.
- Your state or local Builders Association and/or Remodelers Council.
- Your local Better Business Bureau.
- Consumer action lines and consumer reporters. Check with your local newspaper, TV, and radio stations for contacts.
- Local dispute resolution programs.

Miscellaneous Consumer Protection Advice

The consumer protection bureau provides protection for you whether you have a problem with your health club, with an unethical business group or with getting credit.

Health Clubs[xxxvi]

- Within three (3) days after signing a contract, you can cancel your membership for any reason. Cancellations must be in writing, and after receiving your written cancellation notice, the club has 30 days to refund your money

- At any time during your membership, if your contract runs for more than a year, you can cancel by giving 30 days written notice.

- If the health club closes permanently, and the owner does not have a comparable facility within 10 miles of the club, you can cancel and receive a pro-rated refund of your initiation fee.

- If equipment or services that were promised in the contract are not completed by the date specified in the contract, you are entitled to a full refund of your membership fee.

Business Opportunity?

Business opportunities--enterprises which enable you to start a business through the purchase or leasing of equipment or training--are governed by the Small Business Association's Laws and Regulations. This law does not cover purchasing a franchise, which falls under the Franchise Investment Protection Law (RCW 19.100). Franchise purchasers do not have a right to cancel under that statute. If you have a complaint, you can file it online at http://www.consumerprotectionagency.us/. Let me tell the experience my husband had with a "business opportunity."

My husband is someone whom I consider to be pretty smart, ended up in one of these unethical business groups. It started off when he became interested in making some money when he was unemployed from his regular profession for a short period of time. He was always interested in finances and became involved in what I'll call the NVG Financial Group. The person who introduced him to the group said he could make a lot of money selling IRA's and insurance. He thought it sounded pretty good, especially after they showed him paperwork that made them look legit. Then, they started asking him for money. First, they asked him to buy some learning material up front. And, he thought, OK, that makes sense. Then, he was required to go to meetings every week where he was supposed to learn the ins and outs of the business. But, he couldn't sell anything until he got licenses and such, which of course he had to pay for and would take some time to get. This, may not sound too shady to some, but read on, and you'll understand why I grew quite weary of this company. Next, they told him he had to go along on 10 sales calls in order to gain experience in selling financial products.... And he had to provide the names of people to whom to make these calls. Now, that meant he had to give them the names of our friends and family in order to "learn" the business. All the while his manager would be making money and my husband wouldn't make a cent. I was my husband's (and his manager's) first customer and found that I had to pay a good deal of money to invest my money and then I had to pay more money every year to keep my money invested. That just didn't seem right. At this point, I did not want to have my friends and family deal with this company. My husband continued to attend the weekly meetings (which sounded more like pep rallies than training sessions) and pay his fees, until eventually he realized he would not make much money with this financial group.

This business was not one that could be considered illegal and did pass all the business laws and regulations, but still it was a type of organization that should be watched out for.

xxxviiGetting Credit

There may come a time in your life when you wish to go back to school, remodel a home, or get a small business loan. The Equal Credit Opportunity Act (ECOA) ensures that all consumers are given an equal chance to obtain credit. This doesn't mean all consumers who apply for credit get it: factors such as income, expenses, debt, and credit history are considerations for creditworthiness.

The ECOA protects you when you deal with any creditor who regularly extends credit, including banks, small loan and finance companies, retail and department stores, credit card companies, and credit unions. The law covers anyone involved in granting credit, such as real estate brokers who arrange financing. The law also protects businesses applying for credit.

Though you may be hungry for that car, a creditor must live by the rules when they loan money.

When You Apply For Credit, A Creditor May Not...

- Discourage you from applying because of your sex, marital status, age, race, national origin, or because you receive public assistance income.

- Ask you to reveal your sex, race, national origin, or religion. You may be asked about your residence or immigration status.

- Ask if you're widowed or divorced. When permitted to ask marital status, a creditor may only use the terms: married, unmarried, or separated.

- Ask about your marital status if you're applying for a separate, unsecured account. A creditor may ask you to provide this information if you live in "community property" states: Arizona, California, Idaho, Louisiana, Nevada, New Mexico, Texas, and Washington. A creditor in any state may ask for this information if you apply for a joint account or one secured by property.

- Inquire about your plans for having or raising children.

- Ask if you receive alimony, child support, or separate maintenance payments, *unless* you're first told that you don't have to provide this information or if you don't rely on these payments to get credit. A creditor may ask if you have to pay alimony, child support, or separate maintenance payments.

When Deciding To Give You Credit, A Creditor May Not...

- Consider your sex, marital status, race, national origin, or religion.

- Consider the race of people in the neighborhood where you want to buy, refinance or improve a house with borrowed money.

- Consider your age, unless one or more of the following is a fact:

  ➤ You are too young to sign contracts, generally younger than 18 years of age.

  ➤ You are 62 or older, and the creditor will favor you because of your age.

Mindful Note

Your age can be used to determine other factors important to creditworthiness. For example, a creditor could use your age to determine if your income might drop because you're about to retire. It is also used in a valid scoring system that favors applicants age 62 and older. A credit-scoring system assigns points to answers you provide to credit application questions. For example, your length of employment might be scored differently depending on your age.

When Evaluating Your Income, A Creditor May Not...

- Refuse to consider public assistance income the same way as other income.

- Discount income because of your sex or marital status. For example, a creditor cannot count a man's salary at 100 percent and a woman's at 75 percent. A creditor may not assume a woman of childbearing age will stop working to raise children.

- Discount or refuse to consider income because it comes from part-time employment or pension, annuity, or retirement benefits programs.

- Refuse to consider regular alimony, child support, or separate maintenance payments. A creditor may ask you to prove you have received this income consistently.

A Special Note to Women

A good credit history—a record of how you paid past bills—often is necessary to get credit. Unfortunately, this hurts many separated, divorced, and widowed women. There are two common reasons women don't have credit histories in their own names: they lost their credit histories when they married and changed their names, or creditors reported accounts shared by married couples in the husband's name only.

If you're divorced, separated, or widowed, contact your local credit bureau(s) to make sure all relevant information is in a file under your own name.

If You Suspect Discrimination...

- Complain to the creditor. Make it known you're aware of the law. The creditor may find an error or reverse the decision.

- Check with your state Attorney General to see if the creditor violated state equal credit opportunity laws. Your state may decide to prosecute the creditor.

- Join with others and file a class action suit. Contact one of the following organizations to find others to help resolve your issues:

  - Single Women's Alliance Network (http://www.swantimes.org) The Single Women's Alliance Network (SWAN) is a nonprofit organization based in New York City whose mission is to serve the interests of the single woman by providing services, resources and information that promote an independent and secure lifestyle.

  - Alternatives to Marriage Project (http://www.unmarried.org) The Alternatives to Marriage Project (AtMP) claims to be a national nonprofit organization advocating equality and fairness for unmarried people, including people who choose not to marry, cannot marry, or live together before marriage.

- Bring a case in federal district court. If you win, you can recover damages, including punitive damages. You also can obtain compensation for attorney's fees and court costs. An attorney can advise you on how to proceed.

- Report violations to the appropriate government agency. If you're denied credit, the creditor must give you the name and address of the agency to contact. While some of these agencies don't resolve individual complaints, the information you provide helps them decide which companies to investigate. A list of agencies follows.

What to do if You Have a Problem Getting Credit

If you cannot get satisfaction, consider contacting the following organizations for further information and assistance.

- If a retail store, department store, small loan and finance company, mortgage company, oil company, public utility, state credit union, government lending program, or travel and expense credit card company is involved, contact:

Consumer Response Center
Federal Trade Commission
Washington, DC 20580.

- The FTC cannot intervene in individual disputes, but the information you provide may indicate a pattern of possible law violations that require action by the Commission. If your complaint concerns a nationally chartered bank (National or N.A. will be part of the name), write to:

  Comptroller of the Currency
  Compliance Management
  Mail Stop 7-5
  Washington, DC 20219.

- If your complaint concerns a state-chartered bank that is insured by the Federal Deposit Insurance Corporation but is not a member of the Federal Reserve System, write to:

  Federal Deposit Insurance Corporation
  Consumer Affairs Division
  Washington, DC 20429.

- If your complaint concerns a federally chartered or federally insured savings and loan association, write to:

  Office of Thrift Supervision
  Consumer Affairs Program
  Washington, DC 20552.

- If your complaint concerns a federally chartered credit union, write to:

  National Credit Union Administration
  Consumer Affairs Division
  Washington, DC 20456.

Who Are You Going to Call (If You Have a Consumer Problem)?

There are a number of agencies that can help you if you are having most any type of problem.

- Call your local U.S. Post Office and ask for the Inspector-in-Charge if you have a problem with your mail.

- For problems with mail/telephone orders only:
  Direct Marketing Association (DMA)
  1111 19th Street N.W.
  Washington, D.C. 20036

- The Direct Selling Association (DSA) can help you with your complaint if the door-to-door seller with whom you have a problem is a member:
  Direct Selling Association

1776 K Street N.W.
Washington, D.C. 20006

- If you're not sure what federal agency has jurisdiction over your inquiry or complaint, contact the Federal Information Center (FIC), listed in the U.S. government section of phone books in major U.S. cities. For a complete list of FIC numbers, either visit their website: http://www.pueblo.gsa.gov/ or send a postcard to:
  Federal Information Center
  Pueblo, Colorado 81009

Refer to the sample below when writing your own complaint letter.

(Date)

(Your Name)
(Your Address)
(Your City, State, Zip Code)

(Name and title of Contact Person)
(Company Name)
(Street Address)
(City, State, Zip Code)

Dear (Contact Person):

On (date), I purchased (or had repaired) a (name of the product with the serial or model number or service performed). I made this purchase at (location, date, and other important details of the transaction).

Unfortunately, your product (or service) has not performed well (or the service was inadequate) because (state the problem).

Therefore, to resolve the problem, I would appreciate your (state the specific action you want). Enclosed are copies (copies, NOT originals) of my records (receipts, guarantees, warranties, cancelled checks, contracts, model and serial numbers, and any other documents).

I look forward to your reply and a resolution to my problem, and will wait (set a time limit) before seeking third-party assistance. Please contact me at the above address or by phone (home or office numbers with area codes).

Sincerely,

(Your name)

(Your account number)

Canceling a Contract

To cancel one of the contracts allowed by law, fill out one of the cancellation forms given to you at the time you signed the original contract. If you weren't given one or can not find one, write a letter to the company explaining that you want to cancel the purchase. Keep a copy for your files.

Mail the notice or letter to the company by certified mail and request a return receipt. This will confirm that the company received your notice. Be sure the notice is postmarked before the deadline for cancellation.

Five Steps to Manage Your Investments

Sometimes deciding where to invest large sums of monies can feel like a shell game. This will briefly describe the steps to take to help you invest your money wisely (or at the very least to have some savvy before you talk to your banker or a Financial Analyst).[xxxviii]

Mary's Experience: I was the person who handled the finances when I was married, so I don't think I handle them differently then before. However, I wish I had done more financial planning earlier because I would have saved more. Unfortunately when I got divorced I was the only support for two children, so I didn't have much money left to save.

1. Look at the big picture.

2. How much of a risk do you want to take?

3. Where do you want to put your money?

4. Repeat steps 1 through 3.

5. Are you happy with your investment?

Deciding where to put your money can feel like a guessing game unless you get some help.

1. Look at the big picture.

Your initial first step when deciding on investing your money is to look at the big picture: How much? What kind of risk? How long do you want to invest for? To set an investment policy, look at the money you have and decide what you want to do with it. Take your time planning on where to invest your money. People on the average spend a year planning an 8-hour wedding, but less than 1 day planning for a possible 30-year retirement. When you set an investment policy ask yourself the following questions:

- **How much money you wish to invest?** The amount of money you wish to invest may include all or part of any lump sum payment, 401(k) roll over or any other money you may have saved.

- **How great a risk you wish to take?** You can choose a high-risk investment that has the potential for high growth, but also a potential for a great loss. Or, you can choose a low risk option which does not have the potential for such a high growth, but the potential for a great loss is minimized. In general, the higher the risk you take, the greater the potential for gain (or loss).

- **How long a period of time you want to invest?** Do you need easy access? In general, the longer the period of investment, the greater the potential for gain. But, you will not have easy access to your funds in case of emergency or you may have to pay a penalty for early withdrawal.

2. How much of a risk do you want to take?

Now is the time to get involved with your banker or financial analyst. They can perform an investment process called a *security analysis* when they analyze how safe your money is in a particular type of investment. There are two fundamental approaches to security analysis: technical analysis and fundamental analysis. Technical analysis involves studying stock market prices in an attempt to predict future gains or losses. Fundamental analysis involves analyzing the current status of the stock.   Look at stocks for items you are interested in. For example, if you are interested in donuts then look at investments that have to do with donuts.

Companies such as Primerica   can provide you a free financial analysis. This analysis will review all of your current finances and make suggestions, based on your needs, on where you should invest your money.   In other words, if you don't understand anything that I'm talking about here, find a good Financial Analyst, and keep asking questions until you understand what they are saying.

Mindful Note

Remember, a Financial Analyst usually gets paid a commission based on the amount of money they invest for you.

To find a good Financial Analyst contact your local bank, talk to a friend, or refer to one of the following websites:

- **Wise Advisor.com**
  (http://www.wiseadvisor.com/find_advisors.asp?code=gu) Claims to have a sophisticated matching system designed to objectively pair individuals quickly and easily with the ideal advisor to meet each individual's unique needs. They say it's free (but watch those hidden costs) and confidential, takes just 1 minute, and there's no obligation.

- **Investment Counsel Association of America** (ICAA)
  (www.icaa.org/html/cicp.html) Founded in 1937, the ICAA is national not-for-profit association whose membership consists exclusively of federally registered investment adviser firms.

When considering a prospective financial advisor ask the following specific questions:[xxxix]

- What are your qualifications?
- Do you understand my attitude towards risk?
- May I see a sample of a completed financial plan?
- What services will you provide and how often?
- What fees or commissions do you charge?
- Can you provide references

Remember, don't let anyone push you into investing your money into something you don't understand or don't want to do.

3. Where do you want to put your money?

Portfolio construction involves specifically identifying where to invest your money as well as determining how much money to put in each investment choice. This is a personal choice and should be discussed in detail with your investment advisor.

4. Repeat steps 1 through 3.

The fourth step, *portfolio revision*, concerns periodically repeating the first three steps. You may change your mind about your investment objectives, which in turn means that your current portfolio may no longer be the best for you. For example, when you get another job, you may want to re-invest your money into longer-term options.

5. Are you happy with your investment?

The fifth step of the investment process, *portfolio performance evaluation*, involves periodically determining how your investment performed, not only in terms of how much money it made, but also in terms of how much risk you experienced. Are you happy with where you have put your money? For example, if you invested in Sweetheart Donuts and you are having heart palpitations each time the donut market falls one point, even though you are still making lots of money in donuts - is it worth the risk to your emotional and physical well being??? This might also be a good time to evaluate your investment analyst. Do you like them? Do you trust them? Do they do what they say they are going to do? At the very least – do they show up on time??? This is a time not only to evaluate how your money is doing, but how your analyst is doing.

Periodically evaluate how your portfolio is doing...

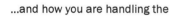

...and how you are handling the  ride.

More Places to Get Help

Several government agencies and business organizations register, regulate, investigate or monitor companies and individuals who offer investment opportunities. If you have questions about a company or an individual, or you wish to make a complaint, contact one or more of these offices, as appropriate. When you seek information, understand that the absence of complaints filed with governmental and private agencies does not mean that a company or an investment is necessarily sound.[xl]

- Federal Trade Commission (www.ftc.gov/): Find publications with advice on avoiding scams and rip-offs, as well as tips on other consumer topics.

- North American Securities Administrators Association (NASAA) (www.nasaa.org): NASAA is the oldest international organization devoted to investor protection.

- Chief United States Postal Inspector (www.usps.com/websites/depart/inspect/aboutus.htm): The Postal Inspectors job is to protect the U.S. Postal Service, its employees and its customers from criminal attack, and to protect the nation's mail system from criminal misuse.

- Commodity Futures Trading Commission (www.cftc.gov/cftc/cftchome.htm): Protects market users and the public from fraud, manipulation, and abusive practices related to the sale of commodity and financial futures and options, and fosters open, competitive, and financially sound futures and option markets.

- Securities and Exchange Commission (SEC) (www.sec.gov/): The SEC's primary mission is to protect investors and maintain the integrity of the securities markets. They oversee key participants in the securities world, including stock exchanges, broker-dealers, investment advisors, mutual funds, and public utility holding companies. Each year the SEC brings between 400-500 civil enforcement actions against individuals and companies that break the securities laws.

- Better Business Bureau (www.bbb.org): The Better Business Bureau (BBB) system in the U.S. extends across the nation; coast-to-coast, and in Hawaii, Alaska, and Puerto Rico. The BBB claims that the majority of marketplace problems can be solved fairly through the use of voluntary self-regulation and consumer education. The BBB's services include dispute resolution, truth in advertising and consumer and business education.

- National Fraud Information Center (NFIC) (www.fraud.org/): The NFIC's mission is to give consumers the information they need to avoid becoming victims of telemarketing and Internet fraud and to help them get their complaints to law enforcement agencies quickly and easily.

Your State Attorney General's Office is also an excellent source of help. Each state's Attorney General[2] Office is sworn to uphold the laws that protect public interest, in specific the Attorney General's Office:

- Works to ensure that families have access to information that promotes the safety, health, and welfare of children in homes, schools, and neighborhoods.

- Protects consumers' access to quality health care services.

- Is a voice and an advocate for seniors, as well as the investigation and prosecution of crimes against them.

- Safeguards consumer rights or getting money back for consumers who have been the victims of unfair or deceptive business conduct.

- Enforces state and federal civil environmental laws to protect and preserve the environment.

- Investigates and prosecutes violations of state criminal law, promotes effective law enforcement and criminal justice, crime prevention, and provides assistance to crime victims.

- Finds more ways to ensure that the civil rights of people of color, the gay and lesbian community, individuals with disabilities and members of other under-represented groups are protected and that they are provided equal justice and equal opportunity.

- Represent the public interest in the proper use and solicitation of charitable funds

Now That You've Stood Up to Those Bullies...

Now that you know how to buy a car and stand up to those bullies who try to get more money out of a job poorly done, it is time to go and have some fun. The next chapter will provide various fun activities for you to do as a single person. Did you think you had to wait for a partner to take that dream vacation? Well, there are travel agencies who can help you plan your trip, with other like-minded singles if you'd like. Ready, set, let's go!

---

[2] The information presented concerning the State Attorney General's Office was obtained from the Massachusetts Attorney General's web site. Although each state's Attorney General's responsibilities are similar, refer to your particular state's web site for specifics.

Chapter 3 Living Now

"The secret of health for both mind and body is not to mourn for the past, worry about the future, or anticipate troubles, but to live in the present moment wisely and earnestly."

Original Buddha
(Hindu Prince Gautama Siddharta, the founder of Buddhism, 563-483 B.C)

The number one important thing about being single is to value yourself, regardless of where you are at. There are days, I know, when you sit around your house or apartment and think of all the things you do not like about your life. You may think "I'd be so much happier if I was married, or if I had a boat." Well, this chapter won't talk about whether or not you should get a boat, but it will help you to enjoy life whether you are single or not. This chapter supports you in resolving the issues of being single and helps you find ways to enjoy who you are now.

- I want to go on a vacation, but I don't want to go alone.

- Going to see my family is a real downer, all they seem to ever be interested in is "when am I going to get married?"

- I spend so much of my time alone, or doing things with my same friends, I get bored. How can I meet new people (both male and female) who have my interests?

- How can I feel better about being single in general?

If you let it, this can be the most exciting, growth-oriented time of your life. While you may not have a partner to share this time, you can find many things to enjoy and emotionally prosper. In this chapter, you will find ideas and activities that show you how to grow intellectually and emotionally during this period when you are surviving being single.

Vacation Alone, With a Group or With One Other Person

You have a job you love. You have friends with whom you share your time, your joys and your sorrows. You have lots of activities you enjoy. But, here comes vacation time. Or, even a long weekend. Dread fills your heart. What are you going to do? Sure your friends share some of your interests, but do you really want to spend seven days alone with Sally or Jack? I don't think so. Even if you do enjoy all the same activities, and can enjoy being with each other 24/7, coordinating vacation schedules can be all but impossible.

It is said that a vacation is a necessary cure for the ailments of the daily routine of life. This is a time to look at your interests beyond your day to day activities. Think about what you want to do with that free block of time and find a way to do it. I'll list some ideas, most of which I found on the internet. In this section, you'll see options to travel single, with a group, or with people of similar interest.

Mindful Note

I met someone recently who said they had gone on a cruise by themselves and was paired up with another single person. They did not get along with this person, and thought of never traveling alone again. I suggested to them (as I am to you), do not base any of your decisions because of one experience. Chances are the next roommate she has will be one with whom she shares many travel experiences.

Have fun traveling alone or with a group.

Travel with a Group

If you want to travel with a group of other singles then check out the following websites which advertise tours for singles:

- Club Med (www.clubmed.com)

  Club Med has 100 so-called villages sprinkled around the world. It offers all-inclusive vacation packages for singles of all ages. Lodging and entertainment are covered in one all inclusive price. I have friends who have gone to one of these villages and they totally enjoyed themselves.

- Match Travel (www.MatchTravel.com)

Provides vacation and adventure travel opportunities for single and solo travelers. Of note: this site is sponsored by Match.com

- Singles Cruises (www.cruisingforlove.com/)

  Cruises geared toward single people and single activities, such as single get togethers, and ice breakers. Cruise to tropical Caribbean, Mexican and European destinations. This company claims that singles travel and cruises are the best way to meet other like minded singles.

- Singles Tours (www.tourgroups.com/singles/opendoor.html)

  Specializes in single tour groups for those between the ages of 35 to 55 to Cape Cod, MA, they also have specialized tour groups for Jewish singles.

Travel with People Who Share Similarly Interests

For those of you who are looking for a vacation that specializes in a sport, hobby or religion check out the following web sites:

- Italian and Mediterranean Cooking Course (www.italiancookerycourse.com/)

  Italian or Mediterranean cooking classes given in the Cantina of an old recently restored large Tuscan villa.

- Vail Mountain (www.vail.snow.com/pb.tips.singles.asp)

  Ski Vail Mountain, with or without an itinerary.

- Singles Adventure Tours (www.singles-cruises.com/)

  Though they call themselves "adventure tours", this site mainly caters to cruises for the single over 40 crowd.

- InfoHub Travel Guide (www.biztravel.com/)

  Whatever your hobby may be (they claim), you will find a like-minded traveler here to share your passion. Packages include travel to Ireland, the Middle East and even Nude Bike Riding tours!

- Cruises for Single Christians (www.adammeeteve.com/pages/christiancruises.html)

  Offers trips for Christian singles to Hawaii and the Caribbean.

- TrekAmerica (www.trekamerica.com)

  TrekAmerica tempts travelers away from the "package" holiday approach and into the world of active and exciting small group adventure holidays. TrekAmerica specializes in "off the beaten path" adventure travel across the Americas.

Traveling Alone

Let's say you do not like groups and just want to go alone. First of all, please be aware of your safety, whether you're traveling in the US or abroad, keep yourself out of harm's way. For example: do not try to save money by staying at the cheapest hotel. That hotel may also be in the worst neighborhood. I'd say if you are planning on traveling alone instead of just checking it out on the internet, check with a travel agency, which can refer you to safe, affordable places to stay.

Mindful Note

There's a possibility the traveling group that you're looking for is right under your nose. Look into whether a local sports or other type club offers trips. Of course, remember you will be spending most of your time doing the sport. So, if you are only a casual biker, unless you like to bike for something like six hours a day, this option may not be good for you. On the other hand, if you love to participate in your sport all day long and are looking for other avid sports enthusiasts like yourself – go for it, it could turn out to be one of your favorite vacations.

Healthy Vacations

If you are a health conscious individual whose idea of a vacation is to come away feeling relaxed, pampered and healthier, then going to a health spa is the place for you. There are hundreds of spas around the world just waiting for you to say "I'm yours". The following sites may offer a link to your dream vacation:

- Canyon Ranch (www.canyonranch.com/)

  Located throughout the US, Canyon Ranch offers a variety of classes, workshops and consultations where you can focus on health issues, combating stress, weight management or a variety of other wellness concerns.

- Destinations Spa Group (www.destinationspas.com/)

  The purpose of a destination spa is to educate men and women about health enhancement through coordinated and facilitated physical fitness activities, wellness education and special interest programming and healthful cuisine. Find links to healthy vacations and self-improvement spas at this site.

- Spa Finder (www.spafinder.com/)

  Whether you're in search of stupendous hiking, a romantic atmosphere, vegetarian cuisine, or spiritual pursuits, Spafinder has hundreds of resorts listed alphabetically and described by category.

- Kripalu Center for Yoga and Health (www.kripalu.com)

Located in the Berkshires of Massachusetts, Kripalu offers a reasonably priced place to stay. They not only offer yoga classes, but also classes on self-discovery, holistic health and spiritual programs.

I'm So Bored

Are you one of those people who frequently have those days when you say "I'm so bored!!! I have nothing to do. I have no one to do it with. My life is such a drag." I think these days are the toughest, especially if it is also raining (you know what I mean!). So, what do you do? I'd say – have a back up plan. Ok, so all of your friends are busy – or your closest friend with whom you always do things just met someone and is spending all their time with them. So ... what do you do? During one of those times when you are feeling great (or at least good) about being alone make a list of the activities you like to do by yourself. I will list some suggestions here, but think of your own, make your own list, add to this list. And, when you're having one of those "I'm so bored, no one loves me days" take out this list, go, have fun and be your own best friend.

You can always find some flowers to pick (if you look for them).

Go Somewhere Nearby

A person can feel isolated pretty fast. Especially as a writer, I spend lots of time alone, and I have to sometimes force myself to make contact with people. But, getting yourself dressed and out among people can soon assuage any lonely feelings. Here are some obvious and not so obvious suggestions for spur of the moment activities.

- Go to a museum. Improve yourself intellectually. Museums contain a wealth of beauty, history and other information and are located all over the place. I live in a small town but still within 15 minutes there are three museums (an Art, a History and a Plane museum). What are YOU interested in? I bet you can find a museum for it.

- Go to a new city. Get a map and take a walking tour.
- Look on the internet and find other places to explore.
- Go to the mall and window shop (or people watch).
- While you're at the mall, find a good book or magazine – and read it.
- Take a drive to no place.

I guarantee you, after you've gone to one of these places, your spirits will be brighter and higher.

Take a Walk

As I mentioned walking is one of my favorite things, when I feel bored and am in need of something to do. I put on my shoes and walk out my door. Sometimes, I may even get in my car and drive to a park. Of course, now that I have a dog, I have a great walking companion, always ready and willing to go. When I get home, I don't feel bored any more!

Do Whatever

Mary (my friend, whom I've mentioned previously) is divorced and has been single for a few years and enjoys her own company. When her kids were young she would spend most of her time taking care of them. But, now that they're grown she has learned to fill her time by going out to movies, plays, and exercise classes. She is on many different boards for her job and other interests. Mary has always been a role model for me in that where I am uncomfortable going certain places on my own, for example a restaurant, Mary has no qualms. In fact, she just brings a book and reads while she eats or enjoys people watching. Here is a short list of other activities you can do by yourself to enjoy yourself and life:

- Go contra dancing
- Go skating
- Go swimming
- Draw a picture
- Read a book
- Watch a video
- Go to the movies

Fix-up Your Home

If you don't feel like going out, what about staying home and working on that home project you've always been thinking of doing? I know in my home there are always many things that need to be done, such as tightening the screw on the kitchen cabinet door or putting up a shelf in the bathroom. I find that when I was in my "poor me, I'm so bored;" frame of mind, I couldn't see the cabinet that needed to be fixed. Then, one day, I decided to write all the things I wanted to do around my apartment. I went room by room, listing what needed to be done – get a new lampshade, clean out my bedroom closet, somewhat small inexpensive activities, but tasks that needed to be done. One by one my list grew. The next time I was bored and having the *poor me's*, I pulled out the list and fixed or organized something *(or decided I wasn't bored enough to take on an activity)*. It gave me a great sense of satisfaction as I crossed a task off the list and I felt competent as I looked at my completed project.

You do not have to be a master carpenter to be the fix-up person around your home.

Your home can be anything from a one bedroom apartment to a 9 room house; either way I'm sure there are things that you want to do to improve it. Again, this is another sub-list for you to make and have handy for when you are having one of "those" days. A sample list is shown in the next figure.

To Do List

Tighten screw on
   kitchen cabinet door
Change oil in car
Paint living room wall
Clean bedroom closet
Organize office file
   cabinet

Never Be Lonely Again

In the previous section we covered activities you can do on the spur of the moment, particularly when you are having one of those down days. Now we'll discuss even more activities you can do, so that you will have fewer of those "I'm so bored, no one loves me" days. I used to feel that way especially on Saturday nights. "Another Saturday night and I don't have a date. No one loves me." Then, I discovered contra dancing. There was a gathering every Saturday night in the town next to me. I love to dance, but didn't like to go to singles dances. At Contra Dances I found that people just dance with anyone or dance alone. You did not stand out like a sore thumb when you sat down alone. You were just resting from having so much fun dancing. I soon found that Saturday nights did not have to be lonely nights any more. I could go out and dance and have fun (without the pressure of having to meet someone). Let's see if some of the following suggestions spur you into finding your "Contra Dance".

Have Fun and Exercise at the Same Time

Most of us want to be healthier, and we know exercise is the way to go. But, when we hear exercise – we think – boring, painful and just another thing you *have* to do. But exercise can also mean, getting out there and having fun, such as:

- Canoeing
- Golfing
- Bird Watching
- Hiking
- Tennis

- Swimming

- Biking

- Volleyball

Whatever your delight, get out and try it. The best way to get that exercise is to do something you enjoy – try them all, it's never too late to see which one(s) you love.

Join a Group

Maybe you might want to add to that sport by joining a group of people who are interested in the same activity . . . or not. What else are you interested in: cooking, reading, playing chess? There is probably a club to meet your every interest. And, I mean getting out and meeting people at the club and entering into their activities. I do not mean sitting at the computer and joining an on-line club, although those can be fine in a pinch, there is nothing like face to face contact with people who have similar interests. I am going to list some clubs here just to get you thinking. Remember, join a club where you are going to enjoy the activity (not just because it may be a good place to meet a partner.)

- Biking, Skiing, Rock Climbing

- Professional Organization: e.g. Society of Professional Engineers and Teachers Unions

- Sewing, Knitting, Embroidery

- Cooking, Baking, Craft Making

Look on the internet (or at the library if you do not have a computer at home) and enter the name of what you like to do the most, and I'm sure you'll find a club that is in your neighborhood.

Get the Theatre Bug

My friend Mary became involved in her local theatre and she has met people, has fun, and she does something she loves. Mary happens to be interested in acting, so she performs on stage. But, there are a lot of other types of jobs that are required in plays also: stage production, set design, advertising, etc. Mary has found theatre people to be energetic and fun to be around. She has the theatre bug and she loves it.

Take a Course/Teach a Course

When I mention course here, I mean any course you take where you learn something new. This could be a college course or an Adult Education course. What do you want to learn? Do you want to advance in your career? Do you want to learn how to make pottery? Can you gain rewards from learning how to handle your stress better? Have you put off getting that advanced degree for too long? People who are in their 60's and 70's are getting their degrees these days – it's never too late. Go to your local library and tell them you want to take a course in a certain subject and they can point you in the right direction.

Also, what about teaching a course? I'm sure in all your years you have found out something that not too many other people know and would like to know. Get together an outline for that class and call your local adult education to see if they also think it is a good idea.

Be a Foster Parent

So you like children. You are a loving, patient person. Then, think about becoming a foster parent. The National Foster Parent Association (NFPA) is a nonprofit, volunteer organization. Some interesting facts about being a foster parent:

- Although you can pick the age of a child, you may find that you are most effective in caring for a specific age group or a range of ages.

- The length of time a child stays in your home is generally limited. The goal is to seek a permanent placement for the child as quickly as possible, whether it is reunification with the birth parents, relatives, or adoption.

- Single persons and married couples are generally accepted as foster parents. Some states do not license/certify homes in which unmarried adults are living together unless they are relatives.

- In most states foster children are eligible for Medicaid cards that cover medical, dental and counseling services.

- Generally, the requirements to become a foster parent include:

  - Age 21 or over

  - Regular source of income

  - No felony record on police reports

  - Home assessment of all family members

  - Attendance at training sessions

- Foster parents receive a reimbursement that is intended to cover the cost of food and clothing for the child. Some states provide a clothing voucher at the time of the child's first placement. Others provide clothing vouchers at the beginning of each school year.

- In most cases, foster children can share a bedroom with another child of the same sex.

Being a Foster mother can be a most rewarding challenge.

The first step in becoming a foster parent is to obtain an informational booklet at the following website http://www.nfpainc.org/Inquiry.html or by calling the National Foster Care office at (800) 557-5238.

Be a Mentor

If you cannot commit your home and time to live with a child, then try being a mentor. A mentor is someone who cares, listens and offers encouragement to children. One of the most effective ways to help young people overcome challenges and achieve their potential is through mentoring. Mentors come from all walks of life and are of all ages, but they share a commitment to making the world a better place for children.

A child and their mentor are matched up by personalities, interests, and needs. They do activities together such as talking, playing sports, or reading together. By volunteering an hour or two a week you can have a great impact on a youth. Usually a year's commitment is required.

For more information or to locate mentoring in your area either call toll-free 1-877-BE-A-MENTOR or visit www.mentoring.org.

If you are 50 years old or older you may want to participate in Save the Children's Intergenerational Mentoring Activities. The goal of the 50Plus Mentoring Program is to create a structure within which children and trained older adults can make long-term commitments to work together and to learn from one another. Mentors help with academic growth, support the development of each child's individual abilities and promote social skills and healthy behaviors.

Get In Touch With Your Spiritual Side

Whether you're Catholic, Buddhist, Jewish or Presbyterian your religious organization is always looking for people to help out. This help may be in the form of organizing a trip, teaching religious education or cleaning the activity hall. By participating in activities with others who share your spiritual interests, you can develop yours more deeply.

My friend Sue gained much satisfaction by teaching a religious education class. Through the research she was required to do, she learned many of the basics about her faith with which she was not familiar. She found she was able to relate on a deeper level with others of her faith. Therefore, by teaching this class she felt less lonely and more connected.

Help Someone – Volunteer

There is no better way to appreciate what you have than by helping someone who has less than you do. When I volunteer, I feel more encouraged than the person I helped.

You do not have to be a genius or have plenty of time to bring joy to someone by volunteering.

Do not volunteer to make others feel better than you, volunteer to make yourself feel better than you feel now. Here's a short list of the type of volunteer opportunities needed by the United Way:

- Distribute Food Boxes to people living with HIV/AIDS.
- Be a trail walker for the Audubon society and assist sanctuary staff in keeping abreast of trail conditions, reporting natural history sightings, act as an on-trail Audubon presence and resource for sanctuary visitors, and reinforce sanctuary policies.
- Drive/Escort individuals who are blind. Bring them to their appointments and/or food shopping.

- Become a Data Entry Clerk with the Camp Fire Girls.

- Want to work with kids, but cannot commit too much time. Rock and feed babies or play with pre-school age children at the YWCA's drop-in centers

For a list of volunteer opportunities close to you visit www.volunteersolutions.org.

What Do You Say When Asked – Are You Seeing Someone?

Is it a good idea or a bad idea to visit your family when you are feeling lonely? I have found that visiting my family can make me feel a bit more depressed. I mean, if I go and see them, usually the first question they asked is: "Are you seeing anyone?" Yah, right. If my answer isn't "Yes, I'm seeing this wonderful person" I have somehow failed their social test. And, let's say I tell them the real answer, "Me and that loser boyfriend Jack just broke up." They still immediately ask: "Have you met anyone else?" or they question my judgment by saying "Oh, but he was so nice, that's too bad."

If you get along with your family (or can at least tolerate them) and haven't seen them for a while, then hey, give them a call and when they ask a dreaded question try giving them one of the following responses.

Question # 1: Are you seeing someone?

Response: Yes, I'm seeing someone; I'm seeing my dog, my landlord, my friend Mary and the people I work with. Is that what you meant?

Question #2: When was the last time you had a date?

Response: Well, I had one with breakfast this morning.

Question #3: When are you getting married?

Response: When I find someone who doesn't drink, is employed and hasn't had a recent emotional breakdown.

Question #4: You'd better get married soon, or all the good ones will be taken.

Response: I think all the good ones were taken when you married mom.

Question #5: When are you going to give me grandchildren?

Response: I can run down to the sperm bank and give you one in 9 months. Is that soon enough?

Question #6: What happened to that nice girl Rosie?

Response: She was really a prostitute and she went back with her pimp. She was just posing as my girlfriend, so that you would not ask Questions 1 through 5.

Question #7: Why aren't you married?

Response: I want to be like (choose one of the following individuals who are single or were married past 40):

> Greta Garbo

> George Clooney

> Helen Hunt

> Sandra Bullock

> Cat woman

> Buddha

> Aphrodite

> The Lone Ranger

> Superman, Wonder Woman, Dudley Do-Right, etc.

Become Your Own Best Friend

I was at a fund raising walk the other day and I ran into a woman named Paula. In the midst of a pleasant conversation, I told her I was writing this book. She was over 40 and had never been married. We started talking about what she did with her time, if she wanted to be married, etc. She seemed like a very happy, attractive, together person. She told me she loved her time alone. She frequently did things (like this walk) alone, but always ended up meeting interesting people. She didn't feel that she would meet so many people if she was partnered up – or even had been doing the activity with a friend. She loved doing things by herself. She explained to me that she had lots of friends, but it was frequently so complicated making plans. For example, to do this walk, she just had to take a left turn on the highway, when she was coming down from seeing her sister, and here she was. She liked the spontaneity of doing things on her own.

Many unattached people that I've talked with feel the same way. They may even add that having a partner has hindered them from doing the things they really want to do, because they always have to take the other person's needs into consideration.

I'd say Paula and the others who think this way are their own best friends. They enjoy their own company, they enjoy getting out and doing things alone – but they also enjoy being with people at times.

Live Your Life

Life is not about sitting around and wondering when I am going to meet someone. Nor, is it about making money and then using your spare time to spend that money. Life is about enjoying yourself and helping others to enjoy their lives. Whether you choose skydiving or hiking the Appalachians, find time to help others enjoy themselves too, by providing encouragement to the next person jumping off that plane or by mentoring a child who needs some extra help with their homework. You have gifts to give. You have things to learn. Get out there. Enjoy yourself, today. Do not let the fact that you do not have a partner stop you from living the life you want.

If you have any interest in finding a partner, the next chapter is for you. It will (in conjunction with the affirmations and meditations in Chapter 5) describe how to find a partner in a mindful way. First it will help you decide what qualities you want in a partner. Then it will educate you in the different ways to meet that person. Finally it shows you the best (including safe) ways to enjoy that first date.

Chapter 4 "Meeting" Someone

"You yourself, as much as anybody in the entire universe, deserve your love and affection."

Original Buddha
[Hindu Prince Gautama Siddharta, the founder of Buddhism, 563-483 B.C]

Now that you know that you are not alone as a single person (in fact 40% of the population is single) and that the reason your parents may bug you about getting married is because the average marriage age was so much younger during their time, you should feel less pressure to get married. In fact, now that you can hire a contractor and go on a vacation, you may wonder "Why do I really want a partner?" That is a question that should be mindfully resolved by looking into yourself using one of the meditations described in the last chapter of this book. If you decide you are interested in looking for a partner, how do you do that mindfully?

As you may have noticed, this book is not about *finding* a partner - it's about thriving during the time you are between partners and making the decision as to whether you *want* to have a partner.   But, of course, a book about being single cannot be written without putting in a chapter about finding a partner, in this case, finding a partner mindfully by first thinking through, then acting on the following questions:

- Where can I find a mate?
- What qualities do I really want in a mate?
- How do I write a good personal or on-line ad?
- What types of information should I find out when I first meet someone?
- What types of questions will they ask me?
- What should I do before, during and after the first date?
- How can I handle rejection?

Deciding When/If to Partner Up

Before experimenting with ways to meet someone, it is important to examine your motivations to partner up. Becoming involved with the wrong person or before you are ready to be in a committed relationship can lead to life long unhappiness. The old adage that "it is better to have loved and lost than never to have loved at all" does not work when the person you partner up with is mistreating you or is just not ready for love.

Though we receive a lot of peer and family pressure to partner, it is really *our decision* whether we form a relationship or not. It may be a good idea at this moment to pause and evaluate why you are not in a long-term relationship right now. Hmmph – I know if someone said that to me when I was single, I would think, "It is because I am out of shape" or "I have some type of inherent flaw that keeps others from wanting me." In my heart I knew these statements were not true, because I looked around and saw the ugliest, meanest, most horrible women married. So, again, I asked myself "Why am I not married?" For me, it was because I had been hurt in my previous long term relationships and I did not want to be hurt again. It wasn't until I could resolve in my head and heart, that I could have a happy relationship, one that did not contain the flaws of my previous ones, that I realized I did want a partner.

So, what may be internally keeping you from partnering up?

The answer may be as simple as not wanting to give up your lifestyle, like my friend Kathleen: "I like my freedom. I don't like the idea of having to answer for where I've been or what I am doing." Or, maybe you feel like Karyn, you don't have the confidence that you will find the right partner: "I don't feel that I'll ever find the right person for me. I just don't think it's possible. So, I guess I'd like to be married again, but I won't take that chance again. " Can you relate?

How do you feel about yourself and relationships in general? A deep part of you may feel that you don't deserve or can't sustain an intimate relationship, or that it will turn bad like some of your other relationships have. The meditations and affirmatinos presented in Chapter 5 of this book will tell you how to look at these feelings and turn them around. It will help you come to realize you deserve a partner and can have an excellent intimate relationship if you decide you want one.

Mindful Note

If your decision is that, at this moment, you would like to put yourself out there again, then try some of the methods suggested here. I believe, your intended will come in the time decided by the universe (but that's a whole 'nother book!).

It's ultimately your decision whether you marry or not.

How It's Different Dating Past 40

Whether you are back on the dating scene after a long relationship (or marriage), or have continued dating throughout your 20's and 30's, and have just not found the right person, you may notice that dating in your 40's or later can involve the following nuances. I've also provided some suggestions on how to deal with them.

- As a man or woman moves along in time and through relationships they acquire the battle wounds of dating. They may have been burned by cheating or lying lovers. Other lovers may have dropped them without notice. This may cause them to take more time to trust that wonderful you who will not lie to them. They may need to be doubly certain that when you say you are working late, that is the truth and you are not really out with "the other man (or woman)." Have patience, on both sides. Try to recognize each other's fears and see each person as a unique individual, different from your previous lover.

- The older a man or woman is, the more difficult it may be to open up to a dating partner and develop an emotionally intimate relationship. This may have been caused by previous lovers/friends to whom they opened up and who then betrayed their confidences. Let your new partner know that you will cherish their secrets…and be sure to keep them secret. Remember, a confidence told to you by another, does not mean you share it with your best friend. It means, you take the confidence and hold it dear to your heart, being proud of yourself that your partner felt safe enough to share this private thought with you.

- If you are single and never married, you may tend to cut out some of the most suitable over-40 dating partners who may be widowed or divorced. Don't count a person out just because of their previous marital status. The widowed or divorced individuals have the long term experience on how to deal with a relationship – they (hopefully) have learnt how to compromise, and how to recognize that when another person complains it is not directed at them personally. They may have the experience understanding the nuances of a relationship, such as how a female is different emotionally from a male, or how it takes work to grow and understand another human being. Even if a person has had a bad marriage, there were many skills they have learnt on how to deal with a relationship. Someone who has been married before generally is not plagued by fear of commitment. So, even though you may prefer someone who has the same previous marital status as you, take another look.

In summary, when seeking a new partner, keep an open mind. Use the check list provided later in this chapter and if a person meets most of the qualities you are looking for, but has been married or doesn't seem to open up so easily – give them a bit more time.

Who Are You Looking For?

When you are seriously looking for someone it is a good idea to have in mind what type of person for whom you are searching. Appendix C provides a table for you to use to rate approximately 50 personality characteristics of a potential partner. Complete this table to determine what is important to You!!!

Mindful Note

Don't expect to find someone with all the qualities you are looking for; 80% is a general rule.

So find some time when you can really think about who You are and what You need (want) in a mate. Have fun and be honest when completing the table.

Especially for You

Whether you're single because you were never married, are divorced, etc. there are special circumstances that affect you.

Especially if You're Widowed

The bad news is that research has shown that widow's bodies often close down when their husband dies. They feel numb, and at the same time, may also have sexual feelings that manifest in aberrant ways. Others feel what can only be described as lots of "crazy emotions." All of a sudden and for no apparent reason, widows may fantasize about having sex with their neighbor and then feel scared of this feeling.

According to psychoanalyst John Hassler of La Jolla, California, it is common for young widows to have a series of sexual encounters. These affairs give widows permission to feel and reaffirm their aliveness.[xli] Regardless of their situation, experts recommend that widows/widowers not move for at least a year after their spouses die. Some of the reasons they give for not moving on for a year are shown below:

1. You must sort through the issue of whether or not you are feeling you are being unfaithful.

   When you date initially, you may feel like you're betraying your spouse. Try to give yourself some time to think why. Are you making yourself feel guilty, or are other people making you feel guilty? You may even feel like a traitor and liberated all at the same time. Listen to your own heart and try to follow what you feel is right. Don't think about what he would have wanted, or what others want for you. Focus on your own needs.

2.   You have to come to grips with sexual memories of our deceased spouse.

Do not rush out and date if memories of your deceased spouse engulf you. To the extent that these memories allow you to think about what kind of partner you may or may not want to have now, they are helpful. Calling them forth in helpful ways allows you to move on.

3.   You have to be careful not to let others exploit you.

Be careful not to be taken advantage of sexually, emotionally, or financially. If you choose to seek out others through personal ads or over the Internet, be extra careful when you arrange to meet, and under no circumstances should you offer to pay their way. If you decide to use a dating service or join a singles group, do a background check on the organization - get references; check their status with the Better Business Bureau.

The desire to overcome loneliness is a major task facing widows. Each will confront it in her own way. Some plow full speed into business ventures or return to school, others find comfort in the company of other widows and single women friends, some widows' venture into the dating world. As with anything, and the basic message of this book, date when you want to, date when you are ready, but either way live your life fully.

Especially if You're Divorced[xlii]

If you're divorce is final, you're no longer concerned about the impact on your court case, except to the extent it might be used against you in a custody fight. You can now focus on whether dating is right for you. You should begin to date when *you* decide it's time to date. Don't let other people rush you. Don't let other people slow you down. You do it when it feels right for you.

And do it with the person who feels right for you. Resist the temptation to find somebody who's totally different from your ex-spouse. Remember, there were a lot of things about your ex-spouse that were appealing at one time. If you're attracted to people who are different, that's fine; just don't feel that you can't date someone who has anything in common with the person you once loved.

Your First Relationship

There's a special role your first love plays after divorce. It can be a time of delightful discovery, a chance for you to rediscover your playful side, to have some fun. Your first relationship though will almost never be a stable long-term relationship. I don't know why. It just is. The first serious relationship you have after divorce will be wonderful, and hopefully you'll look back on it with pleasure and gratitude. Just don't expect it to be the basis of your next marriage. Enjoy your first relationships after divorce. They're part of the healing process. Just resist the temptation to jump in irrevocably. You're probably less ready than you think.

Dealing With Your Children

Remember, your children have gone (or are going) through the same grieving process you did, and they may be at any number of points in the process. Just like you did (and maybe still do); they may jump wildly to different points. That's their job.

What that means, of course, is that there may come a time when they want to be supportive of your moving on with your life, but they simply can't bring themselves to support it. Quite unintentionally (or maybe intentionally), they will sabotage your dating plans. They will whine when you're on the phone, misbehave when your date arrives, fail to give you messages, and otherwise throw a wrench into your best-laid plans. Understand that this is neither malicious nor uncaring on their part; they are dealing as effectively as they can with their grief over your separation and divorce.

So what can you do? Mainly, be patient. Make it ever so clear that your dating is an adult issue, that your date would never and could never replace their other parent. It will take far longer than you would like, and there will be promising improvements followed by disappointing setbacks. Eventually, your children will come around.

Especially if You're Gay

While evidence of gay relationships have existed in society since 2400 B.C.[xliii] many people are still struggling with it, as exhibited by the political battle of legalizing gay marriages. But, in fact, gay and lesbian couples seek the same kind of mutually supportive, romantic, and emotionally intimate bonds as straight couples. They struggle with the same issues of finances, intimacy, and extended family as straight couples. While gay relationship satisfaction is largely the same way as well, McWhirter and Mattison[xliv] discussed the different concerns a gay relationships may have:

- Role identification
- Family acceptance
- Higher incidence of HIV/AIDS
- Fewer role models
- Questions about their sexual orientation

Mindful Note

I am sorry to say that while researching this book, I was not able to find any dating tips for gays. While you may see I found tips on other types of relationships and heck there is a lot out there on HIV/AIDS (not to minimize its importance), I could not find any tips on how to meet a compatible, nice, gay partner. Since many of my gay friends appear to have the same dating issues I had, I will assume, for the purposes of this book, some solid information and help can be found out of this book no matter what sexual orientation you are.

Thoughts on Dating After 40

When I was 28, I ended a long-term relationship (actually, he broke up with me). I was single again. While I was devastated about the end of the relationship, my sister (who was married at 19) started calling me an old maid. The last thing I wanted was to be an old maid. As one by one my friends married, I continued dating, still carrying the old maid sign. I honestly felt I was the bridesmaid who was never the bride, since I was in four weddings. When I was in my 30's, I fell in love with someone I thought was the one. He was successful, handsome, had been an Eagle Scout (one of my criteria at the time) and had a great body (one of my other criteria). He ended up being an abusive alcoholic. I stayed with him for six years, mainly because, when I was with him, I was not an old maid. I was someone who was with someone. I stayed with this man who was abusive, and cheated on me, just not to be alone. Now, of course I look back on that experience and realize how dense I was, but the Old Maid sign was something I dreaded like the plague.

Today I know that getting married is not the be all and end all, and having the Old Maid sign on my chest, is really not a bad thing. As I described in Chapter 1:

- People are marrying later
- More people are not marrying at all
- People are having children on their own
- More people are divorcing (which makes more people single)

But, still most people generally want an intimate partner, it's part of our inbred genetics: marry and procreate. It is with this knowledge that we should take a deep look inside and see if we agree with these statements:

- I realize it would be OK to be single the rest of my life.

But...I am lonely, some of the time.

And...I would rather be with someone – possibly married, or in a serious relationship.

Dating while complicated and difficult before 40, gets more so after that magic number. First off, there's the pure act of finding someone who wants to go out with you (and that you want to go out with). Then, there's the getting to know them. At first we are all on our best behavior, so it is hard to figure out who a person is and if we can deal with their foibles. By the time we see their problems we are attached to them (or at least what we want of them) and do not want to break it off. In fact, usually, when we see their foibles, they apologize and say: "I will never do it again. Which is the first step in changing a person (but that's a whole other story).

Dating Rules After 40

If you have been out of circulation for a while you may find dating rules have changed a bit:

- On the first few dates, people take separate cars. This is in case the date turns out to be a disaster; they do not have to worry about how to get home.

- You do not tell a person where you live for the first few dates. Again, if the date is a disaster or they turn out to be a stalker or some such dangerous type person they cannot come after you.

- First dates usually happen over lunch.

- Who pays for the date is unclear. This needs to be discussed. As a general rule, each pays for their own expenses, at least for the first few dates – then some serious discussion needs to take place as to who pays what.

- Does the man hold the door for the woman? Try it and look for her body signals. If she likes it, then continue doing it, she may think you are treating her special. If she doesn't like it, stop doing it. She may want to feel more independent.

Finding a Partner

When I was single, I frequently heard: "Have you met anyone?" Well, the fact of the matter is, there are many places to "meet" people. I mean, you must "meet" people every day. The point is to meet the right person, have the chemistry work and find the time to be together to grow the relationship. It is only after I went through these three steps that I felt comfortable saying that I truly "met" someone. This section will describe how to find people to meet. If you get to the point of telling others you "met" someone that is up to you (and your potential partner.) But hopefully you are living life like Eva who went to singles dances, but got quickly bored. So she decided to live her life focusing on doing the things she enjoyed like swimming and going to museums. She did many activities for personal growth, realizing that if she met anyone it would be a bonus. Eva did end up meeting her second husband after she turned 40 through a blind date set up by her daughter.

Blind Dates

I sometimes watch the TV show "Blind Dates." It seems there is always a similar pre-dating pattern and dating:

- Person A suggests to person B that they want them to meet Person C.

- Person B and C are both hesitant about going on the date, then each give in and agree reluctantly to the date.

- Expectations grow in both persons B and C. People they tell (esp. family) get excited about the date, further building person's B and C expectation.

- Before meeting their prospective dates, persons B and C fantasize about each other.

- They meet.

At this point, they may either like or dislike one another. The odds are they will not be a match. This may be because each person's expectations grew too high before even meeting. Don't expect perfection from yourself or your potential new soul mate. No one will ever measure up to your concept of perfect and guess what... you will never be perfect either.

Mindful Note

Don't expect chemistry the first date. Try to make having similar interests and hobbies your second date criteria, not physical appearance or chemistry.

Blind dates are opportunities to meet someone special.

Blind dates can be awkward — and sometimes downright uncomfortable, because you are with someone you don't know. Also, you may feel pressure to be liked, so the person who fixed you up does not lower their opinion of you. If the person turns out to be a poor match, the date can become even more difficult. However, these kinds of dates are opportunities to meet wonderful people and possibly even the right mate. Refer to The First Date on page 67 for hints on meeting your blind date and you may just find your match.

Personal Ads: Print or On-line

I want to say up front here, I met my husband through a personal ad, but I'll talk a little about that later. You can find personal ads everywhere these days, both in newspapers and on the internet. They all work basically the same. You enter information about yourself which is then placed either in a newspaper or on the web for others to see. There are numerous web sites, many catering to the over 40-age group. Do an internet search on *40* and *dating* and you'll come up with a whole slew. I've listed just a few, including a description found on their web site.

- **Eharmony.com** Participants take their time and fill out an in depth and rigorously defined profile. Every match is screened for compatibility with you, so you don't have to search through endless profiles. Definitely for people who are looking for a serious relationship. (Heterosexual only.)

- **Soulmatch.com** Claims to be the first online dating site focused on values, faith and the search for Spiritual Chemistry. Designed for both the spiritual dabbler and the devout their questionnaire helps you express your personal beliefs and values, saying just how important they are to you.

- **GayMatchMaker.com** Claims to be the original online matchmaking website designed for the Gay, Lesbian, Bisexual, and Transgender community. Every member's profile and photo is verified through a two-step computer and human screening process to ensure legitimacy and seriousness.

- **Date.com** Participants must also complete an in depth profile, though not as rigorous as Eharmony.com. Although they are a site that boasts it is for people looking for a casual, pal or serious relationship they also say that they average approximately 50 marriages per year. Date.com also holds social events.

- **Match.com** The well known Forbes magazine rated Match.com as one of the best dating service sites around. It has one of the largest memberships going.

- **Widowsorwidowers.com:** This site is especially meant for single widows and widowers. The site states that registration is free and it allows you to search and browse for members. Once you find a match you can send them a message.

- **PrimeSingles.com** Specializes in over 40 singles, their friend finder technology helps you create a personals profile and find singles based on your personal preferences. Prime Singles claims to provides comfortable, safe and reliable dating and match-making services. Build your personal ad free and enjoy live chat, message boards, a photo gallery and more.

When trying to find your partner let them know who You are – Not some image of who you want to be.

Although on-line dating services, request that you fill out a form with your information, other personal ads require you to create a short description of yourself. If you are looking for someone who is interested in You...your mind, heart and spirit, in addition to how you look, then both your personal and on-line ad must be crafted to reflect who you are.

- **Be Honest.** The fastest way to ruin what might have been a beautiful friendship is to lie. Hide the fact that you are a single father of 5 year-old triplets, and you miss a chance to find the woman who wants to love them and share your parental joys.

  Dishonesty will always be found out sooner or later. Allow others to make informed decisions about what they will and will not accept, based on an honest representation of you. Open yourself to incredible happiness by allowing others to love you as you are, for who you are. In other words, in the ad, say who you are today - not who you want to be, or who you were 20 years ago, but who you are today. When I was dating, I frequently met people who said they liked to do a certain sport, and but when it got down to details it turns out they hadn't actually done the sport for more than 10 years.

- **Create an Eye Catcher.** An attention-getting headline stands out above the rest and demands to be read. There are many, many 'DWM's, 44, seeking love' out there. Be different, even if you are a 'DWM, 44, seeking love'.

  Check out the competition. What attracts your attention to their ads? Note that those which stand out are clearly written, are original, personal, and direct. What can you say about yourself in a single sentence that makes you irresistible to a potential partner, or at least exemplifies your best qualities?

- **Be Specific.** You know who you are and what you want…tell them about it! Almost everyone seems to enjoy 'moonlit walks, candlelight dinners, and strolls on the beach'. Be specific about your values, in addition to naming hobbies and interests. If you know your soul mate is a Buddhist, say so. If you spend most of your time rock climbing, convey that too. What is your personal mantra? Share it. The person, who understands and appreciates it best, is the one who will reply. Refer to the checklist you created on page 70 and put in some of the 5's.

- **Be Positive.** Find your natural exuberance and zest for life and let it shine through in your writing. Negativity repels.

- **Be Honest, Be Honest, and Be Honest.** One aspect that cannot be over-stated!!

Mark's and Valerie's Meeting

This is a very personal story of how I met my husband when I was 43 years old.

Valerie's Story

I had tried blind dates, going to single dances and even hooking up with dating agencies in my search for a partner. This time I decided to put an ad in an on-line dating site. It was 1994 and there were not as many on-line dating services as there are now. Basically, the ones that were available were associated with a newspaper. The ad I wrote would appear both on-line and in hard print in a local newspaper.

I had responded to personal ads in newspapers. Although the men I met were nice enough, there was no connection. I therefore decided to place my own ad. With this new ad, I wanted to be perfectly honest with what I wrote. I really wanted to attract someone who would like me – at least like the few characteristics I described in the ad.

> ### Let's Talk and Hug ...
>
> & play and be best friends. I'm 43 into yoga, meditating, x-country skiing, rollerblading, happiness, honesty and trust. Seeking someone compatible, around my age, who lives in Metrowest area.

Valerie's Personal Ad

Along with this ad, I was also permitted to record a phone message. I repeated what I said in the on-line ad, with a few other personal qualities including that I worked for a large computer company.

A little more than a week later, I called the number the dating company had given me and heard the response from Mark. He said he liked to cross-country ski, meditate and a lot of the other things I said. He said he worked for a large computer company too. I also received a response from one other person. This other person mentioned a bunch of things they liked, but not one interest was the same as the ones I had put in my ad. I wondered, had they even read my message? Needless to say, I called Mark and that was the beginning.

Mark's Story

Mark was driving around one night feeling lonely and ended up in a convenience store in a nearby town. (Coincidentally, near to where my sister worked and where he would eventually rent his tuxedo for our wedding.) He picked up the newspaper where I had placed the ad and drove home. At home, he browsed through the personal ads. When he saw my ad, (he says) it appeared 5 times larger than all the other ads. He liked what he read. He put the paper down on his table. Now, Mark is a bit of a paper pack-rat. He accumulates mail by the ton. Well, one would think that this newspaper would get lost in his pile - but no - the paper (with the ad showing) "kept rising to the top as he puts it." Finally, about a week later, he called the number to listen to my voice message. He was even more intrigued, and left a response; including his phone number.

Valerie and Mark

Well, it turned out that not only did we have in common the qualities I mentioned in the ad, but we also worked for the <u>same</u> large computer company. We talked many times on the phone before meeting. I did not give him my phone number (or even the city that I lived in) until we met at which time I saw him as interesting, attractive and compatible. We married a year and a half later.

Dating Agencies

Dating Agencies are companies that match individuals with others using "computer-based" criteria. Usually you pay a set fee to meet a certain number of people. I am going to tell you my unhappy story, though I'm sure that others have had a better luck.

I had quite a busy life. I was meeting men, but not anyone I liked or they did not share my interests. I saw an ad on TV for (what I'll call) Meet Your Match. It said that because matches were made by entering details about their clients into a computer, the individual you would meet would match your interests. One lunch time I decided to go in and try.

When I arrived at the Meet Your Match office I was surprised it was so small. Since there were so many ads on TV I expected a large enterprise. I was asked to sit in a large comfortable chair. A rather nice looking man (who made me think "if the clients are like him, I'll surely be satisfied") named Al came up to me and greeted me. Al started asking me what I was looking for in a man. I told Al the five major characteristics I was looking for. Al told me, that they match on 100 characteristics. He said I would fill out a form where I would indicate what I was looking for in a man. The form would be run through a computer – and voila, a list of the names of men who matched my interests would be printed. I was enthused, I was looking forward to meeting someone who had the same interests and this process seemed to meet my needs. I filled out the questionnaire. It asked everything from what I liked in my coffee, to what qualities I most desired in a man. After I was done filling out the form, I went into Al's office.

Al glanced over my form, and said, "Offhand I can think of 5 gentlemen clients whom you would like very much." I was thrilled. But ... we hadn't talked money yet. He said for $1,000 he could introduce me to 6 men who would be very close matches for me.

I thought a minute, I hadn't expected it to cost so much. 6 dates for $1,000!!! That was a lot. I expressed my concerns to Al. He smoothly explained to me that the normal cost was $1200 but, if I signed the contract by 5:00 p.m., I would receive the reduced price of $1,000. I weighed the options in my mind. If they could really find a suitable match, the money would be worth it. But, this was sounding too much like a high-pressure deal. He said I had until 5 p.m. that day to think it over.

I left the Meet Your Match office and returned to work. Every now and then, while performing my tasks I thought about the dating service and the possibility of meeting Mr. Right. At 4:30, Al called. I still hadn't made up my mind. But, with Al's convincing I agreed to sign the contract and pay $1000 for 6 dates.

I went home and waited for the phone to ring, telling me that a date was being arranged. One week passed, two weeks, three. I thought: "What happened to those 5 gentlemen that Al said he could introduce me to that weekend?" I called the agency. Al said he was sorry he hadn't gotten back to me. He did have a name for me to consider. He described someone who lived 100 miles away, owned a gun collection (I am an anti-gun activist), and major interest was CBs (I am not interested in CB's at all). I balked, saying that this person was not at all compatible with me. Al said he was sorry and would get back to me in a week. This time a month passed. Finally, Al did call. I decided to talk to the person he suggested. Again, he turned out to have no interests that were compatible with mine, except that he was having the same experience of meeting Ms Wrong through the agency as I was having meeting Mr. Wrong. A few weeks later, I was referred to another 'gentleman'. He also was incompatible, and had none of the characteristics I had indicated on my computer dating form. I called the agency and said I wanted my money back. Al told me I was just being picky and they had referred me to some nice men and I should be more open minded.

Over the next nine months, other men were referred to me. All of them were incompatible. I decided to move on in my pursuit of Mr. Right (or Mr. Nearly Right.), never receiving a refund of my money.

Speed Dating

Fast cars, fast computers, fast life ... what else should we expect now except Fast Dating otherwise known as Speed Dating. Speed dating provides singles the opportunity to date (or at least meet) up to ten or more other singles in one evening.

How is this possible, you ask? Each date lasts approximately seven minutes. What makes speed dating different from the typical bar scene is that participants have the same objective — to meet a potential companion.

The rules of speed dating are quite simple. A group of singles gathers at a cafe or similar venue. Equipped with a nametag, a scorecard and their best personality, people are paired up to begin their first date. Though some speed dating gatherings are different most allow you to discuss anything, except your career or where you live.

Following seven minutes of conversation, a bell is rung, and the men move on to meet their next *date*. Following each *date*, participants mark on a card whether they would have an interest in meeting that person again. If a mutual interest is noted, speed-dating organizers provide each party with the other's phone number.

Speed dating has proven to be fairly successful, with approximately half of all participants coming away with a potential match. While some may be uncomfortable with the notion of making repeated small talk ten times in one evening, advocates of speed dating believe that the success of this "unconventional" arrangement lies in "conventional" — simple chemistry.

But the question remains: Is seven minutes enough time to fairly assess someone? After all, in this short time, you may have written off someone you might have otherwise found interesting in a traditional dating scenario.

Conversely, you may think you've met your dream date. But had you more time — even one more minute — you might have discovered that "dreamboat" has a toe-nail clipping collection under his bed.

However, the popularity of speed dating is growing at a rapid pace.

You can meet a lot of people in a short period of time by speed dating.

Singles Dances

I rarely had luck at single dances. Except for once, I don't really know why, but the night and the light and the stars must have been right for me. That night I had two men virtually fighting over spending time with me. Other than that night, the frequency with which I got asked to dance just seemed to depend on – who knows what. Some nights, I would sit in total embarrassment waiting for someone to ask me to dance – while the friend I came along with got asked for every whirl. Those nights, I would want to hide under the table wishing I had come alone in a separate car and I could leave immediately (preferably by indiscreetly crawling under the tables). Other singles that I have known have the same feeling about these dances. They believe the dances are superficial at best. This is my story of one night at a single's dance.

*The evening starts by getting dressed the best (I mean the best) that I can.
Makeup, clothes, everything – to the hilt!!! Then, I join a friend, whom I can*

immediately see is more sexy and beautiful than I (whether she is or not doesn't matter – the fact was my insecurities were already rising and I feel she is goddam beautiful). Anyway, we compliment each other on how we look and confirm that we are just going to dance. We ride off to hopefully meet our destiny.

Arriving at the dance hall (usually a Knights of Columbus hall) I notice a line of men at the back of the room. They check us out. I suck in my stomach, and quickly find a chair and a drink – not necessarily in that order. I gulp down an alcoholic beverage. I rarely drink, but this is a time I have at least two or three in the evening. I start looking around. I notice one or two men who look appealing (hey, it is time to be superficial isn't it? Looks are mostly (ALL) that counts in this situation). I hope one of those darlings will come over and ask me to dance – or that I get up the courage to go and ask him. After sitting and sipping for a while, I notice one of those hunks (they are quickly rising on my scale of attractiveness) is looking in my direction. I smile broadly – even though my friend is telling me how terrible her boss is – heck this is about meeting men, not listening about bad bosses. The hunk starts walking in my direction. I hold in my stomach and push out my breasts, acting like I don't even notice him walking towards me. I act absorbed in my friend's conversation. He comes closer – and then just when I am prepared to say "Yes, I will dance with you" he stops at the table next to me, bends over and asks THAT woman to dance. My heart sinks.

I take notice of my friend's conversation for real. I realize what I may end up with at the end of the evening is only (I slap myself – ONLY – this person has seen me through hell and high water) this friend. The night progresses. Someone finally saves me from being stuck in my lonely seat of humiliation and asks me to dance – who cares if he is two feet shorter than I and is obviously wearing a toupee – I am dancing. On the floor, I dance my best, thinking how my dancing is so expert, that I should be on TV. I'm sure that the hunkity hunk dancing with that skinny tree in the corner will notice me and want to share my skill (and maybe my body later – yes, yes, yes!!!)

The evening ends. My friend exchanges numbers with a fairly attractive looking guy. As beautiful and as wonderful as I felt when I came to the dance, is not as yucky and ugly as I feel now. As I drive home, I fake complimenting her on her catch, while I am secretly feeling inferior in every way. The fact that they ended up going on only one date and she finds out that he is just barely ending a 10 year relationship, I don't know that now. Because, now all that matters is that someone wanted her phone number, her destiny to marry is still alive – while I go home and cuddle with my cats, and console myself by saying I am just as happy as I am now.

I wonder today, how I would handle single dances. Maybe I wouldn't go at all. But, at the time (before internet dating and the such) that was one of the few ways to meet a partner, especially if you were over 40. Even I will admit, not all dances are so difficult. At one dance I even met someone who I dated for six months. Here are some thoughts on going to single dances:

- Keep your expectations low.

- Realize that some of the people there are married.

- Realize that some of the people you meet tell stories (otherwise known as lies) to impress you.

- Realize that there are some really nice compatible people there – but they may be hard to find.

- Throughout the dance repeat to yourself some of the affirmations suggested in the last chapter of this book.

Still, look put your best foot forward when you go – just in case your soul mate is waiting to ask you to dance.

Meeting on Your Street

There are many other ways to find someone. I like to call it meeting on the street, because you don't go out of your way by putting yourself into situations that are set up specifically to meet someone, instead you meet them where you live and doing the things you like to do. It does require you to get out off your couch and out the door. Find something that you enjoy doing, and do it. If you are serious about meeting someone (refer to the meditations in Chapter 5 to decide this) you should act on one of the suggestions I mention in this chapter at least once a week. That way, you will have the experience of meeting people and be prepared when you find that someone special. Here are some of the ways that you may find your destiny "on your street".

In the Vegetable Department of Your Grocery Store: This is my husband's favorite. He said he actually went on a few dates with people he met while picking out bananas. I guess the routine is to ask some unattached looking person (e.g. no wedding ring) if they think that eggplant is ripe. Then, strike up a conversation.

At a sports or recreation club: How hard can it be to go out and do something you like? Even if you don't end up finding your mate, you will either get some exercise or learn more about something that interests you. I am only going to list a few clubs, but there are really many others.

- Bike

- Photography

- Appalachian Mountain

- Computer

- Nature

- Bird

- Cooking

Look on the internet to find clubs that are closest to you.

- **On-line Chat Rooms:** Be careful, but find a chat room that you are interested in and type away.

- **Classrooms:** Is there something you want to learn? To improve your performance at work? Just for fun? Maybe this is a good time to sign up for a class.

- **Church/Synagogue/Mosque/Religious Center:** Some religions offer single get togethers. Otherwise, volunteer at one of their other activities.

- **Professional Societies:** There is some type of society that represents you. These societies usually provide both informational and networking meetings. In fact, many of them offer an hor d'oeurve and networking hour before the informational meeting.

Be sure what you do is for your enjoyment and not only to meet someone or you can set yourself up to spend a lot of time doing activities you don't enjoy.

The First Date

Congratulations on meeting someone with whom you want to go on a date. Maybe you met them on the internet or at a single's dance, whatever ... the moment has arrived - you are going to go out with possibly Mr. or Ms Right. Before you leave home review your wish list of characteristics that you created in Appendix C, remembering that you will not find out these qualities on this date. The more you are prepared for your meeting - the less anxious you will be about it.

Mindful Note

Though this book will provide ideas for meeting a person for the first time and dealing with the associated stresses, it might be a good idea to find other books that deal directly with dating strategies.

Safety First

Yes, we've come to a screeching halt here... There are too many stories out there about what can happen when two strangers meet. So, before you leave for that date, follow these safety reminders:

- Don't allow yourself to be pressured into meeting anyone. If they threaten to terminate the relationship if you don't meet them within a certain time frame, end the relationship then.

- Meet in a public place. If during the date, you decide to go somewhere else, use your own car.

- Don't agree to hiking dates or meetings in remote areas until you know someone very well. Plan a short initial meeting. If, on meeting, you know you won't be seeing this person again, sharing coffee and a little polite chat won't be as painful as spending a long day together.

- Before you meet them, listen to the "Lessen Pre-Date Jitters" relaxation script described in Chapter 5 of this book, to regain your center and confidence in whom you are. The more confidence you have in yourself, the more confident you will be talking to someone and taking care of yourself.

- If you travel to meet your on-line love, make your own hotel and car reservations and don't give out the name of your hotel. Drive yourself to the hotel, or take a taxi. Provide your family or friends with necessary contact information.

- If you start feeling unsure or uncomfortable about your date, politely excuse yourself and leave by the back door if necessary. Do not hesitate to ask for help from persons nearby. Trust your judgment and don't be afraid of potential embarrassment. Better to be embarrassed than physically hurt.

You won't end up in trouble if you keep in mind your safety.

If you follow all of the previous recommendations, you will feel safe and enjoy your dating experience to the fullest! Be happy, find love!

Dating Tips

I have found it is best to have a plan in mind before going on a date. It prepares me for what may (or may not happen). It also helps me to enjoy the date. So, here are some tips for those of you who are a bit concerned about what to do on that first date:

- **Relax/Breathe.** I can't over-emphasize this enough. Take a deep breath every time you feel anxiety or discomfort. Breathing will bring you back to yourself and your body, making you feel more relaxed and comfortable. Enjoy your date's company and look at the experience as a chance to make a new friend, or to be enlightened on a subject you knew little about before the date. But above all, breathe and relax. Listen to or read the relaxation and affirmation script Lessening Pre-Date Jitters beginning on page 107 in to gain confident throughout the date.

- **Plan your date out ahead of time.** Decide on something and do it. Be open to other suggestions if your plans don't work out. Make sure these plans adhere to the rules shown in the Safety First section on page 86. Just because they seems great in the first five minutes doesn't mean they don't have a dark side.

- **Be well-groomed.** Look and smell the best you can. Remember, first impressions involve what you are wearing and how in general you appear. Wear your favorite outfit. You want your new relationship to enjoy you because of who you are and what you like (and in the first meeting, first impressions of a well groomed person are important.)

- **Pay attention.** Listen and notice what is happening from the first date to whatever transpires over the next few months. Above all, if there are any of the Red Lights listed on page 89 then try to make a gracious exit. But, if you at least kind of like the person, show them the respect they deserve and let them know you are sincere about getting to know them.

- **Be genuinely interested.** Be interested, because you are. Listen to what type of activities this person enjoys. Listen to how they treat people. Refer (in your mind) to the checklist you completed in Appendix C and listen for those cues. If they say they are looking for a person to skydive and you hate to even get into an airplane, then kindly finish the conversation, say it was nice meeting you and skadoodle. Even if they are totally attractive, if you find yourself saying to yourself "well I can deal with that" or "they can change", realize they are not the right person for you and move on.

- **Get past the superficial:** Remember there is a lot more to a soul mate than:
  - ➢ How much money they make
  - ➢ What kind of car they drive
  - ➢ How they dress and otherwise look.

- **Be yourself.** Remember you are not only looking to get to know the other person but you want them to get to know you. Do not say you like to swim when you are deathly afraid of coming within 100 feet of a body of water.

- **Offer to split the bill.** It is courteous to offer to "go Dutch" and you should always be prepared to split the costs. If your date does pick up the tab, offer to pay the next time.

- **Act chivalrous.** Men, the women's liberation movement may have provided women with the means to financial independence and positions of power, but this does not mean that she no longer appreciates those little things that make you a gentlemen. Open doors for your date, pull out their chair, make sure they get home safely. These are the things that make a good impression.

- **Be open to possibilities.** Don't expect to be knocked off your feet. Simply meet the person and be open to the possibility of any connection, whether it is an intimate relationship, friendship, business associate or it may be a person who leads you to your right relationship.

- Don't…
  - ➢ Drink too much.
  - ➢ Talk about your ex too much (more than five minutes).
  - ➢ Expect the male to pay.
  - ➢ Feel obligated to tell your shortcomings.

➤ Monopolize the conversation.

Most Important – Have fun on your date.

After the Date

After the date, sit back and think of how it went and how you feel. Do you have a smile on your face, thinking of some of the things that the other person said, or do you have a sense of dread about when they may try to contact you next. After a date, it's a good practice to do some or all of the following things.

• If this was a blind date, call the person who arranged the meeting and let them know how the date went.

• Review the date in your mind. Think of what you liked and disliked about the person. Refer to the list you created on page 70 and check off the qualities they had that you liked or disliked. Maybe this is a good time to add or subtract from the Worksheet you completed previously in this chapter.

• Pat yourself on the back for all the brilliant answers and questions you presented, and be kind to yourself for all the answers you gave that were not so brilliant.

• Do something nice for yourself.

Red Lights

If you find your date exhibited any of the following characteristics, then please, do not see them again – they spell danger.

• Cruelty, viciousness, as expressed in mockery, putdowns.

• Immaturity, as expressed in "games playing", blame laying, whining.

• Superficiality, as expressed in vanity, flightiness, pettiness.

- Drinks more than two glasses of alcohol with their meal.

- Lacking in wisdom and *common sense*.

- Lacking in integrity and basic honesty.

- Lacking in compassion and generosity.

- Lacking in inner strength (courage).

Listen to what the other person says and pay attention to your inner cues when deciding to continue to date someone.

Dealing with Rejection

No matter how good you looked, or how much you liked the other person, sometimes things just don't work. Who can chemistry? Perhaps it was lack of similar interests -- whatever? The key here is to realize this IS ONLY ONE PERSON, ONE DATE. If you feel rejected, or haven't received that promised phone call or email then take one or more of the following actions:

- Keep your chin up, get right out there and live your life. This book (I hope) is teaching you to live your life fully with or without a partner. Do it. Get off that couch. Put those cookies away. Stop thinking that your cat is all you really need as a companion. You need friends. Get out and do something you enjoy.

- The person you just met doesn't really know you. I mean YOU John Smith or Amy Jones. Do they know how kind you are to animals? How you take your Dad to the cemetery every year, just because he likes to go? Of course not, they just know someone whom they met for one hour or so. One hour of your many hours of your life.

- The other person may have a subconscious reaction to how you look or some phrase you use. For example, you have black hair and for some reason the person is attracted to red heads. Well, you can dye your hair, just so that person may like you, but who knows they may then only want someone who rock climbs and you are afraid of heights. Remember, dating is about personal preferences, chemistry and destiny.

- Use the Re-Center after Rejection from a Partner relaxation and affirmation script that begins on page 111 to help you to focus on and release any "negative" energy you may be holding in when you felt rejected. This script also focuses on incorporating new and positive energy in place of the negative energy.

You've Met Someone!

OK, the Karma is there and you found someone you like. You both have similar interests and the chemistry is there. Congratulations. I think. Now the work has really begun. You have "met" someone. This is the time to really get to know the other person, especially if you want to head toward marriage.

Mindful Note

One other important note, before you have sex, be sure that you both have an HIV/AIDS test. This will keep both you and your partner safe and protected.

Surviving a Breakup

I wasn't planning on writing anything about breaking up after a long term relationship. This was because basically this book is not about long term relationships. But a friend called yesterday and I realized breaking up or ending a relationship, no matter how long or short it was, is an important part of dating. Let me tell you about my friend. First of all, she is the sweetest, nicest, sexiest (men have told me this) person I know who is over 40. To start again, she called yesterday and said this guy she had been seeing for a year and a half had broken up with her on Valentine's Day. I won't even get into the almost inhumanity of breaking up with someone on Valentine's Day, I think we all know what that is about. But, after a nice dinner (that he had cooked) and receiving a card (that said he loved her) and a box of heart shaped candy, he told her he was planning on returning to China. He had been talking with some friends where he used to work, and he decided he needed some space to seriously think about returning to China – alone. My friend asked some questions; mostly starting with the word "Why?" In a daze, she got her coat on and returned home. When she got there, still in a daze and sobbing, she (rightfully so) reached out to her friends.

I think some people minimize the trauma that is caused by a break-up. Suddenly, this person with whom you have talked most every day, spent all your spare time with, and who shared your hopes and dreams is suddenly gone. I mean, let's look at this more closely. What are you left with, after this person says, "good bye – it's not you, it's me?" A major void – that's what you're left with. The phone is not ringing. You have no one to tell about the Blue Herron (or new restaurant or building or whatever) you just saw. You cannot tell your ex-lover (who shared your enthusiasm about birds, restaurants, and architecture, whatever). You feel like no one else you know is interested in those same things. With whom do you go to the movies? Sitting alone on the couch on Friday nights, to whom do you reach out? What about the trip you planned to Bermuda? With whom do you go now? And, finally, what about those dreams of marriage and a family with this mostly wonderful person – what happens to your dreams now?

What happens now is that you look at your life and realize you must start over, and you do. You improve your spirits by using the affirmations and meditations in the next chapter. You start spending more time with your friends. You get re-involved with your old hobbies and activities that you neglected while you were with this person. After a while, you may start to look for a new person, find out about the new person, and build dreams with a new person. You hold on just a little less tight than the last person you dated, because who knows when this new person may just say "I'm leaving for Africa, don't worry, it's not you." You wonder to yourself am I too old (now even though this book is for people over 40, I had this thought at 28) to find someone new? Am I too old to be sexy and desirable?

We all do move on from this breakup trauma. We find books that say we are OK. Our friends say we are OK. We look at our life and see we are OK. We notice that there are other people who are attracted to us. We notice that we are attracted to others. Amazingly, that other person's foibles come to brighter light, and we wonder what we saw in them anyway. We refocus on what we want and need in someone now. As we start to date we see that there are other people with more compatible traits, some who can offer more and that is what we focus on. That is how you survive the breakup.

To Date or Not to Date, That is the Question

You are now armed with all the information you need to decide if dating is for you. Do you like the idea of sharing your life with someone every day? This is a decision only you can make. You now know it is not a necessity to find a partner, but you can if you want. The next chapter will provide meditations and affirmations that will help you through the whole process of deciding whether you want to date, to handling a rejection when a partnership goes wrong. Now, relax with the information you've gathered so far, and move on to the next chapter where you will find some inner support dealing with the dating or non-dating world.

Chapter 5   Look Inside to Find What You Need

"All that we are is the result of what we have thought. The mind is everything. What we think we become."

Original Buddha
(Hindu Prince Gautama Siddharta, the founder of Buddhism, 563-483 B.C)

By looking deep inside, through relaxations, visualizations and affirmations, you can begin to attain the life you want.   Many of us already use affirmations throughout our day such as when we find ourselves saying in our mind "I will do well on this test." We may say this, even though we are frightened that we will not do our best and even though we have studied the material and are well prepared. Using affirmations to help create a life in which we are happier is similar to this example.

Affirmations combined with correct knowledge as I have presented in the rest of this book are powerful tools. If you have done affirmations and found they have not worked, maybe it is because you did not have the facts to back you up. For example, if you believe your mother when she says that everyone is married, your confidence will remain low, no matter how many affirmations say that being single is OK. But now that you know that 1 out of 10 people never marry, and have read the other facts presented in Chapter 1, you can have the confidence to remain single until you decide it is time to marry. You are now armed with the practical tools to take care of yourself as a single person on the outside; now let's see what you want on the inside.

Sometimes we are afraid to admit to what we want, even though in our hearts we know what it is. And, even then we are frightened to go after it. Maybe we have gone to too many single dances and felt rejected or we have been hurt in past relationships. Or maybe we have not accomplished all that we wanted to in our past endeavors and our confidence is low. All this can set up a barrier to letting ourselves know what we want out of our life.

Mindful Note

You can obtain a CD or cassette tape of the guided relaxations described in this chapter in one of the following ways:

Go to the author's website: www.surviving-life-mindfully.com

Send an email to: Survivingbooks@aol.com

Write to: Valerie Pederson-Purinton
               PO Box 254
               Stow, MA 01775

Many people have used meditations and affirmations in different ways as shown in the following experiences. Eva would use them to see the man she would marry in her thoughts:

When I was single, I'd use affirmations and write down my specifications for a mate. With my present husband, during a meditation I felt a voice came from God, my higher power or a higher source that told me how I would meet him.

Mary used them in a similar way:

I guess in a way I have used affirmations in that I have written down in journals what I wanted my future partner to be like.

Have you ever visualized the person you want in your life? Brown hair and brown eyes?

By using the meditations and affirmations in this chapter you can break through barriers, reward your true self and

- Come to believe you deserve the best possible life.
- Get in contact with how you feel about having a partner.
- Overcome negative feelings you have about yourself.
- Reduce the stress of obtaining your dreams.
- Retain hope.
- Gain self-confidence.

Once you have broken through these barriers you will have a better chance of living the life you want. Use the information presented in this chapter to help you decide what *you* want *your* future to hold and learn how to get it.

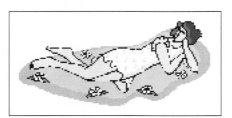

Your dream partner can be just a thought away.

Daily Affirmation

The following affirmation will help you to gain confidence in yourself, like yourself more and therefore find a partner who reflects the best of you more fully. If you want, modify the affirmation to reflect your personal wishes. Begin the affirmation by reading it at least once every day. If you like, write it on a separate piece of paper and tape it to your mirror.

I am beautiful on the inside and out. I do my best to be kind to others. I realize the next intimate relationship I have will be better than the last: There will be more happiness, fewer arguments, more trust. I am releasing any fear I have about getting into another relationship. I see now that I can find the best partner for me. I am meeting more and more eligible people. I am able to judge their compatibility more wisely. I know I will find my match at the right time.

Look Inside for the Life of Your Dreams

The affirmation in the previous section helped you realize you deserve what you want. Now, we will go a bit deeper with a combination of affirmations and relaxation to find the life of your dreams.

This section will help you create a mental picture of the life you want through a deep relaxation. Some people call it a self-hypnosis or meditation. Combined with seeing your actions and goals in your mind - it is called a creative visualization. Buddhists believe that what we truly want in our hearts is what is truly meant to be. But, sometimes, because of incorrect learning we have come to believe we do not deserve what we want or for some other reason cannot attain our dreams. This chapter presents the script for you to record to lead you through a visualization to regain the correct learning and live the life you want. After you create the recording, listen to it as often as possible. Use it to help relax, gain confidence and set and achieve goals.

Mindful Note

The opportunity is presented in this book for you to record your own relaxations If you hear the affirmations with your own voice then the affirmation will go deeper into your subconscious and you will get a better result from it. Of course, you may also buy the recorded meditation. Instructions on how to do this are provided in the beginning and end of this chapter, and at http://www.Surviving-Life-Mindfully.com.

The meditation is divided into the following four segments:

- Relaxation.
- Listening to a Visualization Tape (such as Lessening Pre-Date Jitters on page 105).
- Affirming your life.
- Awakening refreshed and relaxed.

Relaxation

During the relaxation section of this meditation you will be asked to take notice of all the parts of your body. Through the pure act of taking notice, your body will relax. To help this relaxation process you will be asked to visualize yourself melting into a big puffy cloud. During this time, you will also take notice of your breath. You will learn a technique that will help your true self become more connected with the universal energy.

Listening to a Visualization Tape

Creative visualizations help us make our own realities, our own fate and our own luck. Visualization is the technique of using your imagination to create what you want in your life. There is nothing at all new or unusual about creative visualization. You are already using it every day, when you imagine the activities you are going to do this day, or when you see in your mind, your loved ones returning home. It is your natural power of imagination, which you use constantly, whether or not you are aware of it.

You will find within this section five types of visualizations, referred to as "Visualization scripts" that you record along with the relaxation and closing segments of the complete meditation. Each script leads you through a visualization and provides affirmations and suggestions related to the topic. These scripts help you to re-center by

- Noticing and accepting how you feel,
- Releasing any unpleasant, unnecessary feelings that may be blocking you
- Seeing in your mind the best outcome
- Affirming your true self

You may choose which (if any) of the following visualization scripts to insert into your meditation recording. The script and affirmations included for each script begin on page 98. The script topics are shown on the following graphic.

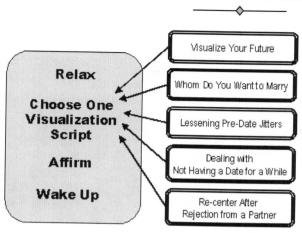

Relaxation and Visualization Scripts

- **Visualize Your Future**: Use this script any time you want. Let it help you visualize a happy, peaceful existence by first focusing on your past accomplishments. Then contemplate the suggestions that help you remove any emotional and physical obstacles you may have to obtaining the life you want, whether single or married. The script concludes by providing suggestions to visualize the details of your new life.

- **Whom Do You Want to Marry?** Use this script after you have consciously decided that you would like to have a committed relationship. Reflect on the type of person with whom you want to be. In this script you visualize this person then realize and remove any emotional blocks to meeting them. This person may be someone you know or someone you do not know. You envision what you and this special person would do together, how you would relate, how they would fit into your life. Use this script to first spiritually connect with the special person, which will lead you to connecting to them in reality.

- **Lessening Pre-Date Jitters**: Use this script before you go on a date. This script first helps you focus on past successful dates. It then brings you through visualizing the details of the current date in a confident, competent manner. It finally guides you through the conclusion of the date. At this point you feel confident and pleased that the date went well. You have found out the information you need to decide if you want another date with person

- **Dealing with Not Having a Date for a While**. If you have not had a date for a while, your self-confidence may be eroding. You may start to think negative thoughts about your life, such as "I will never find someone" or that "I am too unattractive emotionally or physically to meet the right person". This script will help you to focus on and release any negative thoughts and replace them with positive ones. You will find the courage to "get out there" and enjoy life – maybe meeting someone too. You will awaken with a re-affirmed confidence in your skills and goals. This script concludes that when the time is right, you will be living the life that is best for you.

- **Re-center after Rejection from a Partner**. Use this script when you have just broken up with a potential partner. This script helps you to focus on and release any negative energy you may have felt when the relationship ended. It then focuses on incorporating new and positive thoughts in place of the negative thoughts.

3. **Affirming your life.** The Affirmations section of the meditation includes general ideas and verifications that improve your overall self-confidence and self-image.

4. **Waking up refreshed.** The final section wakes you up to a new and brighter day.

General Relaxation

This is a special type of script in that it leaves time open for you to reflect on your own affirmations or suggestions. This time may also be used to meditate on an issue that may be on your mind. During this time of relaxation you are able to ponder any pressing issue with a calmer clearer mind, coming to a decision that is more in touch with your true self.

Some people prefer to only make a General Relaxation recording. In this case, they read the text that contains the affirmations and suggestions before they do the relaxation and let them drift through their mind during the time of silence that is incorporated in the recording.

Relaxation Script

This section presents the script for the primary relaxation portion of the meditation.

1. Record the relaxation script shown in *italic* that begins on the next page.

2. Where it is indicated in the relaxation script record the visualization script, which begins on page 103.

Mindful Note

If you are making a General Relaxation tape, at this point record a two minute period of silence (or relaxing music). Then continue with the next step.

3. Return to the relaxation script, beginning on page 102, and complete your relaxation with affirmations.

Each meditation takes approximately 20 minutes.

Relax, Visualize, Affirm, Wake Up Refreshed

Mindful Note

When you see (pause), in the meditation script, record a quiet moment onto your tape.

Mindful Note 2

When you are ready to start the meditation, find a quiet comfortable spot where you won't be disturbed for approximately 20 minutes. If you wish, you can also record or play relaxing instrumental music while you record or read the script.

You find yourself in a dimly lit or dark room. You are in a comfortable chair or lying down; your back and head are resting comfortably. Bring your attention to your breathing. Notice your breath flowing in and out. . I want you to prepare to take a deep breath now. You will count to five as you inhale and count to five as you exhale. Inhale 2 3 4 5 Now exhale 2 3 4 5. Excellent. Again, Inhale 2 3 4 5, exhale 2 3 4 5. Now, just take notice of the air flowing into your body and flowing out. Do not try to change it or adjust it, just notice it. Bringing in life and renewal, releasing all that you don't need. Now, imagine yourself on a big, white cloud. Above you is a beautiful, clear, blue sky. Bring your attention to your right leg. Lift it up just a bit, then let it sink back into the cloud. Now your left leg, lift it up and let it float down. Your buttocks - tighten and release. Your torso, lift it just a little bit then release. Your right arm, lift it up, let it fall; let it sink into that cloud. Left arm, lift it up and let it fall. Your right shoulder, your left shoulder. Lift your head up, just a bit, and let it sink gently back down. Now, make a face. Scrunch up your face - making everything go toward your nose. Let it go. Open your face wide. Your eyes wide, your mouth wide, open your entire face wide then let it go.

Now again, bring your attention to your breathing. Just notice your breath coming in and out of your body, slowly and comfortably. As you go along in the relaxation you may notice that each time you bring your attention back to your breathing it is slower and more relaxed. You feel calmer and more at peace. If you have any thoughts come into your mind, just let them drift off. Peacefully, let them go. Now remember, here you are lying on this big comfortable cloud, a clear blue sky above you. Do you see it? Do you feel the warm air on you? The sun is gently warming your body. Now bring your attention to your right foot. Notice it melting into the cloud. Now, notice your calf.

Imagine as I go through these parts of your body that you are just relaxing, releasing and letting go, melting into the cloud. And it feels so great just softening. Bring your attention to your right calf. The top of the calf is melting, the bottom - just melting into that great big cloud. Then there's your knee. The top of your knee and the bottom of your knee is softening. Then, your thigh, the top and bottom. Just resting - making more contact with your comfortable spot. You're just like a warm candle melting in the heat. Bring your attention to your left leg. Let your left foot melt into the cloud, and your left calf, the top of the calf and the bottom of the calf. Just sinking and melting. The top of your knee and the bottom of your knee. And then your thigh, notice the top and bottom of your thigh. Now bring your attention to both of your legs. Doesn't it almost seem that both of these legs are sinking deeper into the cloud? The rest of your body will be there soon.

Now bring your attention to your buttocks. Feel the cheeks open up. And your genitals. And your lower stomach. Feel everything just loosening up. Just melting and spreading out. Picture a candle melting on a table and the wax spreading on the table top; that is how it feels with your body, melting and sinking into the cloud. Now bring your attention to your stomach. Let go and feel it spreading and the tension melting away. Sink into the cloud. And then your lungs and your special heart. And your lower back, sinking your whole lower torso sinking and melting into the cloud. Your lower back, your mid back and your upper back. All gently being caressed by this beautiful white cloud. Now bring your attention to your fingers - your right hand. Let it melt. And your right forearm and your elbow and your upper arm. Feel it all melting, sinking into the cloud. Bring your attention to your left hand. And your lower arm and your upper arm. And now your shoulders, feel space being made between your shoulder blades as your shoulders become wider and broader. Wider and broader and softening. And the back of your neck and the front of your neck and the side. Releasing any tension in your entire neck. And, then to the top of your head and the back of your head. Letting any thoughts drift away. And now into your face. Feel your face become soft and subtle. Start with the forehead feel it spread out - and the eyes - especially around the eyes; and your nose and sinuses. Next, relax your cheeks and your lips and your chin and your jaw. Let your jaw gently fall open. You can now feel you are just sinking your whole body is sinking into the cloud and you feel calm and relaxed. You are going deeper and becoming more relaxed and every bit of tension is soon gone from your body.

Now bring your attention to your breathing. For a few seconds be quiet and pay attention to your breath coming in and out of your body. With each exhale imagine any worry just drifting away. Just let the tension go with each exhale. Just gently let it go. Breathe in calmness. Let any thought that comes into your head drift out with each exhale.

Now imagine yourself at the top of an escalator. See it going down in front of you. I am going to start counting slowly backwards from 10 to 1 and when you hear number one you are going to be at the bottom of the escalator and totally relaxed. Again, envision the escalator in front of you. Step on it and feel yourself going down with the movement. 10 - 9 - 8 going deeper and deeper 7 - 6 - 5 deeper into relaxation and calm and peaceful 4 - 3 - 2 -1. You are now perfectly relaxed.

Bring your attention to your breathing again. This time when you breathe; feel a oneness with the universe. Feel the oneness as you breathe. See, in your mind, your breath as a circle. Starting at your lungs see the air come up through your throat, through your nose and mouth - out into the room, into the universe, almost touching the outside of your lungs. Now breathe back in. See the universe's air coming into your nose and mouth, through your throat and back into your lungs. You feel as if your whole life is in balance. Everything is calm and wonderful. You feel totally peaceful, and some things in your life become clear. You love and respect yourself and you know that a higher source is working in your life, bringing you what you need. You feel deep within you that you are a highly intelligent, wonderful person. You know that everything works out for the best in the end.

Bring your attention to your breathing again. Feel that circle, your center, your connection with the universe. Notice your breath leaving your body: lungs-throat-mouth-room, then coming back into your body: room mouth - throat lungs. And, again lungs-throat-mouth-room - room mouth - throat lungs.

INSERT THE TEXT OF ONE OF THE VISUALIZATION SCRIPTS THAT BEGIN ON PAGE 103 HERE. OTHERWISE, IF YOU ARE CREATING A

GENERAL RELAXATION SCRIPT, BE SILENT AND RECORD THAT
SILENCE FOR APPROXIMATELY TWO MINUTES. WHEN YOU LISTEN TO
THIS TAPE YOU CAN EITHER REPEAT AFFIRMATIONS THAT HAVE
BEEN SUGGESTED IN OTHER PARTS OF THIS BOOK, OR YOU CAN
FOCUS ON ANY PRESSING ISSUE OF THE DAY, KNOWING THAT YOU
WILL SEE THE ISSUE WITH A CALM AND RELAXED EYE.

WHEN YOU ARE CUED TO RETURN TO THE RELAXATION RESUME
HERE.

Bring your attention to your breathing again. Your connection to the universe, your center. And feel that circle. The air passing through your lungs-throat-mouth-room - room mouth - throat lungs. Again, feel that circle: lungs-throat-mouth-room - room mouth - throat lungs And, again lungs-throat-mouth-room - room mouth - throat lungs.

Now I am going to say some affirmations that will stay with you. You are a beautiful person. You are beautiful physically, emotionally, and intellectually. God loves you and accepts you exactly the way you are. You love and accept yourself exactly the way you are. Occasionally you make mistakes, but that's OK, you always learn from them. You accept other people as they are; accepting their imperfections, their power to grow and your own power to grow. You feel very calm with yourself and at peace with yourself. You always do what is best for yourself, being loving and kind to yourself first, and then being loving and kind to others. You are an excellent employee. Deep inside you know that you are an excellent and valued individual and employee. You are a wonderful person. You know that everything works out for the best eventually. Therefore, there's no need to worry.

Bring your attention to your breathing again. Feel that circle, your center, your connection with the universe. Notice your breath leaving your body: lungs-throat-mouth-room, then coming back into your body: room mouth - throat lungs. And, again lungs-throat-mouth-room - room mouth - throat lungs.

You feel comfortable and relaxed within your body and within your life. You see the improvements to be made and you are confident that you have the capacity to make the changes.

Right now notice how your body feels, how comfortable, and calm. Notice your thoughts are slow and calm. Notice your thoughts are quieter. I am going to give you the suggestion that whenever you say the word "Peace" you will be reminded about how you feel right now. Your body will know how you feel and you will instantly be calm and relaxed. Say the word "Peace" silently to yourself now - "Peace". Remember the word Peace and your body will be calm and relaxed. Whenever you want to feel clam - say the word "Peace" and your body and mind will remember how it feels now.

Now, if you are going to go to sleep turn off the tape now and drift off into a peaceful slumber. If not, bring your attention to your toes and start wiggling them, bring your attention to your legs and stretch them out. Reach your arms over your head and stretch and you are fully aware and totally calm and relaxed. Open your eyes. Look around and you see the world as a sunny day. You're wide-awake and feeling fine.

Visualization Scripts with Affirmations

This section presents both the meditation and affirmation scripts you can use with your relaxation and separate affirmations that you can use daily. Paste them on your mirror and read them as you brush you teeth. Each Visualization script presents affirmations and general suggestions to give you confidence in coping with your every day life, finding your ideal partner if so desired and connecting with your true self. Choose the script that is the most helpful to you at this moment. For example: If you are nervous about going on a date, then use the Visualization script entitled "Lessening Dating Jitters".

Incorporate the Visualization script into your relaxation in one of the following ways:

- Record, in the appropriate place, the script you will most frequently use

- Record several versions of the relaxation - each with a different Visualization, or

- Record a quiet pause, long enough so that you may read a Visualization script.

Of course, you can use the relaxation without a Visualization script and still receive benefits.

Mindful Note

When you see (pause), in the script, give yourself a few extra seconds to reflect by recording a silent space on your tape (i.e. do not say anything).

Choose the script that will help you make the most of this day.

Visualize Your Future Confidently

Use this visualization script any time you want to feel relaxed and confident. Let it help you decide if you want to marry and remove any emotional obstacles. Examine *if* you want to live with someone. Examine the type of person you want to live with the rest of your life. This script helps you visualize your future life by first focusing on your past accomplishments. It then provides suggestions to remove any emotional obstacles you may have to obtaining the life you desire. It concludes by focusing on suggestions to visualize the details of your new life.

Affirmations

Repeat these affirmations throughout the day to reinforce the suggestions presented in the Visualize Your Future script.

- The life I want is the life I should have.
- I deserve the best possible life.
- There is nothing blocking me from the life I desire.
- I am happy in my new life.
- I am comfortable with the new activities in my life.
- I am happy with the new people in my life.
- I feel a sense of purpose and mission in my new life.
- I know I can be happy whether I am single or married.
- I make the correct relationship choices.
- I am free from any fear in my new life.

Mindful Note

Remember to record the meditation in a calm, quiet, and slow tone of voice.

Visualization Script

You are now perfectly relaxed. Take a deep breath. Count to five as you inhale and count to five as you exhale. Inhale 2 3 4 5 Now exhale 2 3 4 5. Excellent. Bring your attention back to this moment and to your life. Visualize the day you just had. See in front of you the tasks you enjoyed. See yourself working on these tasks. [Pause] Now see the parts of your life you want to improve. Do you want a better place to live? Do you want to be calmer more often? Would you like to have a committed relationship?

What would you be doing right now in your ideal life? [Pause] What does your ideal life look like? [Pause] How would you feel? [Pause] Happy? Energized?

———◇———

Relaxed? Spiritual? (Pause) Ask yourself one thing you would like to improve today? (Pause) How would you do it? See yourself doing it. Can you see yourself doing this activity that brings you more happiness? (Pause) Ask yourself what is keeping you from doing this activity? (Pause) See that emotion, task, obstacle in a bubble. Now, see that bubble floating away, and as it does it pops. And, when it pops you know that that obstacle is not in your life any more. You can reach your goal. You can do anything you want to do to make yourself happy. Ask yourself how you want to live your life. Can you see living your life with a partner? If the answer is yes, then see that partner beside you.

Affirm to yourself that you deserve the best possible life: I deserve the best possible life. Let go any blocks to having the life you want. Let go of any fear you may have of living the life you want. Let go the feeling of not being good enough for the life you want. Realize that you deserve the life of your dreams. (Pause) You deserve the life of your dreams.

Again, in your mind visualize the goal you want to achieve today. See yourself doing this new activity, enjoying this activity and feeling proud of yourself. (Pause) See the people around you, complimenting you. Know that you will get the partner that is best for you. Feel yourself happy and content in your new life. Feel yourself coming home and feeling a sense of purpose and mission in your new life.

Now, complete this meditation by returning to the conclusion of the relaxation script starting on page 102.

Whom Do You Want to Marry?

Use this script after you have consciously decided you would like to have a committed relationship. In this script you will reflect on the type of person with whom you want to be. Refer to the list of qualities that you are looking for that you entered on the worksheet in Appendix C then use this script to meditate on those characteristics you want in a special person.

In this script you visualize this person and remove any emotional blocks to meeting them. This person may be someone you know or someone you do not know. You envision you and this special person together; you sense how you would feel with them beside you. Use this script to first spiritually connect with the special person, which will lead you to connecting to them in reality.

Repeat these affirmations throughout the day to reinforce the suggestions presented in the Whom Do You Want to Marry script.

Affirmations

- I am releasing all negative energy in my body.

- My body is filled with positive energy.
- The right person is coming my way.
- I am an attractive person.
- I am attracting the right person for my life.
- I am now making the best possible choice for my partner
- I feel less and less tense and more and more self confident.
- I am developing an easy going productive attitude towards my search for my partner.
- I know I will find my partner when the time is right.

Mindful Note

Remember to record the meditation in a calm, quiet, and slow tone of voice.

Visualization Script

You are now perfectly relaxed. Take a deep breath. Count to five as you inhale and count to five as you exhale. Inhale 2 3 4 5. Now exhale 2 3 4 5. Excellent. You answered yes, when asked if you wanted a committed relationship; and now it is time to visualize that person. Now, it is time to feel that person in your life. Take a deep breath. Remember the characteristics that you wrote on the work sheet previously in this book. The ones that said what was important to you? Did you want them to be athletic? Intelligent? Well-read? Spiritual? Kind? Take a moment now and review in your mind the most important characteristics of this person. (Pause)

Now, see yourself sitting comfortably in your favorite natural setting: By a pond in a wooded setting? By the ocean? See this special person beside you. You can almost feel their hand. What does it feel like to be with them? Pause a moment and take notice of how you feel. Are you a bit nervous? A bit excited? Are you projecting the negative feelings you had about your last relationship onto this new person? Are you afraid you won't be able to trust this person? Are you afraid that you will not like yourself with this person? Be aware of the feelings you experience when you think about these questions. Notice one feeling at a time - for example if you are feeling rejected - notice in your body how that feels. Notice the possible constriction in your chest, the tightness in your arms, the desire to run and hide. Notice this feeling and realize it is only a feeling. Decide whether you want to hold on to this feeling, to the negative energy. If the answer is no, then release the energy. Release the tightness in your arms, release the desire to want to run and hide. See the feelings floating away. Feel your arms become light as a feather, feel how comfortable you are in your seat. It's as easy as that.

◇

Be at peace again. Take notice of your breath. See it coming in and out of your body. See its circle and your connection with the universe. Notice your breathing again. If an unpleasant feeling comes into your body feel it for a moment and release it, if you desire. Feel the positive energy coming into your body. Remind yourself it is only a feeling. Notice your breathing. Reaffirm that when the time is right to find your partner it will happen and there is no need to feel impatient now.

Now, let's return to this beautiful natural setting. This person, whom you see beside you, is kind and trustworthy. They possess none of the negative characteristics that your previous partner possessed. This person will not hurt you. They will be kind to you in every way possible. You both will be truly glad that you have found one another. You are ecstatic that you made the decision to look for this new person. Take a deep breath. And now another breath, as you sense the safety you will feel with this new person.

You are still at that special place, with that special person. Again, feel them beside you. Feel their warmth. Smile to yourself, sensing how comfortable you feel with this person. Any fears that arise, you let them go. You see these fears in a bubble that immediately pops – and away goes your worry. You are seated calmly and comfortably.

Now, complete this meditation by returning to the conclusion of the relaxation script starting on page 102.

Lessening Pre-Date Jitters

Use this script before you go out on a date. This script first helps you focus on past successful dates. It then brings you through visualizing the details of the current date in a confident, competent manner. It finally, guides you through the conclusion of the date when you feel comfortable and pleased that it went well.

Affirmations

Repeat these affirmations throughout the day to reinforce the suggestions presented in the Lessening Pre-Date Jitters script.

- I remember clearly my past successful dates.
- I am at peace when I meet this new person.
- I feel confident when I meet the new person.
- I will take appropriate actions if I do not feel safe with my date.
- I know I will look my best for the date.
- I feel more comfortable each time I feel the texture of my outfit.

- I am comfortable with what I want and expressing it.

- I become more relaxed as the date progresses.

- I will look for the qualities I want in this person and that will determine whether I want another date with them.

Visualization Script

You are now perfectly relaxed. Take a deep breath. Count to five as you inhale and count to five as you exhale. Inhale 2 3 4 5. Now exhale 2 3 4 5. Excellent. Remember the last date you went on when you enjoyed yourself. Or, even better, remember the last time you went out with a friend and had fun. Maybe you went to dinner and a movie. Did you naturally feel comfortable? Did you naturally participate in the conversation which you and your friend had? (Pause) How were you feeling? Happy? Relaxed? How did you feel after dinner and the movies – just thinking about the taste of the meal or the actors in the movie? Now, take a deep slow breath. Replace the friend with the person with whom you are about to date. See them sitting across the table, maybe the same table where you had dinner with your friend. Remember how comfortable you felt with your friend, you can feel that comfort now – with this new person. When you are on this date, you will find yourself discovering if this person matches what the qualities you chose in Appendix C. You will discover this information during a relaxed, comfortable conversation. Again, feel comfortable.

Imagine the conversation; see yourself being curious about the other person. See yourself calmly, naturally finding out information about your date. Remember the list you wrote? Whenever you feel the conversation lagging, talk about one of your interests from the list, querying your date if they share the same interest. Let them know your interests.

Now, let's walk through the date. See yourself entering the building where you are meeting your date. Feel at peace. Feel yourself taking a long, slow deep breath, remembering how relaxed you are at this moment. See your date coming up to you and possibly shaking your hand. Imagine what your date looks like. See their face and send them pleasant thoughts. Imagine you know this person and you feel safe with them, knowing you are prepared to leave if you do not feel safe. Feel certain that you are prepared for your date. Right now, in your mind, feel the texture of your outfit. Feel at peace - knowing you chose the right clothing and you are neat and well groomed. Know that you look good and feel good. You would not be having this meeting if this other person did not have some interest in you already. See your date asking you questions while you feel competent answering them. See yourself asking questions, finding out what's important for you. Hear what's important for a date. Feel comfortable with yourself and your desires. Bring your attention to your breathing. See it coming in and out of your body. Feel your hand steady and strong. You find yourself answering the questions easily and smartly. Feel the conversation flowing nicely. See the circle of energy as you breathe (pause). See yourself conversing with your date calmly and confidently. Note the expression of acceptance on your date's face. See yourself becoming more confident as your date progresses. See your date respecting your experience. As your date ends, you both rise. You know your date went well. As you leave your date you are confident. Whether you see this person again or not - you feel wonderful. - confident in your personal attraction. You have presented yourself in the best possible fashion. You know that if you do not go out with this person again, it is nothing personal - it is only because your interests did not match and your relationship was not meant to be. See yourself going home feeling comfortable and pleased with yourself.

Now, complete this meditation by returning to the conclusion of the relaxation script starting on page 102.

Dealing with Not Having a Date for Awhile

If you have not had a date for a while, you may feel your self-confidence fading. You may start to think negative thoughts about yourself, such as: you will never find anyone or that you are too unattractive emotionally or physically to meet the right person. This script will help you to focus on and release any negative thoughts and replace them with positive ones. The script also will give you the courage to "get out there" and enjoy life – maybe meeting someone too. It also helps you to re-affirm confidence in your skills and goals. It concludes by assuring you that when the time is right, you will be together with the partner who is best for you.

Affirmations

Repeat these affirmations throughout the day to reinforce the suggestions presented in the Not Having a Date script.

- The life I want is the life I should have.
- I deserve the best possible life.
- I am both physically and emotionally attractive to my future partner.
- I am happy in my life.
- I am comfortable with all activities in my life.
- I am happy with the people in my life.
- I feel a sense of purpose and mission in my new life.
- I know I can be happy whether I am single or married.
- I make the correct relationship choices.

- I am free from any fear of a new relationship.
- I live my life fully and happily.

Visualization Script

You are now perfectly relaxed. Take a deep breath. Count to five as you inhale and count to five as you exhale. Inhale 2 3 4 5 Now exhale 2 3 4 5. Excellent. Bring your mind to the last time you had a date. Think of how long it has been since you have been on a date. Take notice of how you feel. Remember you are not alone. Pause a moment and take notice of how you feel. You may feel unattractive, rejected or shameful. Just feel the feelings. Feel one feeling at a time - for example if you are feeling low self esteem - notice in your body how that feels. Feel the possible constriction in your chest, the tightness in your arms, the desire to run and hide. Feel this feeling and realize it is only a feeling. Decide whether you want to hold on to this feeling, to the negative energy. If the answer is no, then release the energy. Release the tightness in your arms, release the desire to want to run and hide. See the feelings floating away. Feel your arms become light as a feather, feel how comfortable are in your seat. It's as easy as that. Be calm again. Take notice of your breath. See it coming in and out of your body. See its circle and your connection with the universe. Notice your breathing again. If an unpleasant feeling comes into your body feel it for a moment and release it, if you desire. Feel the positive energy coming into your body. Your self esteem is returning. Notice your breathing. You now know that when the time is right to be with your partner it will happen. Trust when the time is right it will happen. For now you live your life fully and happily.

You know you are beautiful on the inside and out. You do your best to be kind to others. You realize the next intimate relationship you have will be better than the last: more happiness, fewer arguments, more trust. You are now releasing any fear you have about getting into another relationship. You see now that you can find the best partner for you. You are meeting more and more eligible people. You are now able to judge their compatibility with you. You realize you will find your match at the right time – realizing that now it may seem a long time coming.

Bring your attention to your breathing. See it coming in and out of your body. See it's circle and your connection with the universe.

Now, complete this meditation by returning to the conclusion of the relaxation script starting on page 102.

◆

Re-Center after Rejection from a Partner

Use this script when you have just broken up with a potential partner. This may be a most difficult time for you. It may be a time when your self esteem may be seriously suffering. You may have the feeling that you will never date again or that this person who just rejected you was the person for you and now you will be alone forever. This script will help you get past those feelings. It helps you to focus on and release this negative energy you may have felt when you were told the relationship had ended. It then focuses on incorporating new and positive energy.

Affirmations

Repeat these affirmations throughout the day to reinforce the suggestions presented in the Re-centered After Rejection from a Partner script.

- All tension is released from my body.
- I feel calm and relaxed.
- I am now available for new better relationships.
- The right person will come into my life at the right time.
- I live a happy and fulfilling life.
- I am free from fear and worry.
- I know that a new person is coming along with whom I will feel accepted, respected and happy.
- I see myself being happy that I am no longer dating the person from whom I just received a rejection.
- I realize that the universe works for me - and I am living a wonderful life.

Visualization Script

You are now perfectly relaxed. Take a deep breath. Count to five as you inhale and count to five as you exhale. Inhale 2 3 4 5 Now exhale 2 3 4 5. Excellent. Bring your attention to the moment you first realized you and your partner were ending the relationship. Maybe it was a phone call; maybe they didn't call for a week (when they previously had been calling almost every day). Where were you? In your mind look around the room. How did you feel? Feel the feeling now. Let it wash over you. See the feeling in your body. Take note of the various parts of your body and how they each felt when you knew the relationship was over. Notice that your fists may be clenched, notice that various parts of your body are tenser -or have more "bumps", feel the feeling and at the same time notice your breath coming in and out of your body, reaffirming that now you are OK and safe. Are your feet a little chilly? Are you feeling a little teary eyed? Does your head ache a bit? Notice these feelings. See them before you. Be comfortable with them. And, then...be assured that these are only feelings and they will pass. Decide if you want to hold onto the feeling. (Pause) Do you want to hold onto this feeling? If the answer is no, then release the tension in your arms; your legs; your torso; your head. Check your entire body and release the tension. Visualize yourself again on the white puffy cloud feeling comfortable and peaceful. Let go of the negative feelings - realizing it is only a feeling. A momentary passing event. Realize you will meet other people. See yourself laughing with your new partner. What is your favorite thing to do? See yourself doing these things you enjoy. See yourself being happy that the old relationship ended, because you know how happy you are now and how happy you can be. See yourself living a happy, fulfilled life. Rejoice, realizing that the universe works for you - and you are receiving all types of wonders in your life right now. Realize that you deserve the best and you are getting the best. Realize that things always work out.

Now, complete this meditation by returning to the conclusion of the relaxation script starting on page 102.

Obtain a CD or cassette tape of the guided relaxations described in this chapter in the following ways:

Go to: www.surviving-life-mindfully.com

Send an email to: Survivingbooks@aol.com

Write to: Valerie Pederson-Purinton
        PO Box 254
        Stow, MA 01775
Enter code #VVVMMM for a $2 discount. Limit 2 per customer.

Chapter 6   It's Your Decision

Deciding whether to marry or not is, ultimately, your decision. I hope this book has provided you with information that will help you to live happily as a single person until you decide whether you want to marry.

Do not rush it. Appreciate you for who you are, partnered or not. Today more and more people are getting married later or deciding not to marry at all -- with all the choices available today, why not? Today, a woman can support herself, heck even have a baby by herself, and for that matter so can a man. Please decide to marry only if you truly love the person and that person makes you feel special. A good sign that this is not the right person is when you realize you enjoy your alone time more than your times with that person. Some people rush into marriage for the wrong reasons, such as it is the right time or their biological clock is ticking, or they feel there is something wrong with them if they are not partnered. Again I say, appreciate yourself partnered or not. Find the joy in your life. Being partnered is not going to make you enjoy your job more (in fact with stresses that may occur in a bad marriage it may make you dislike it more). If you do not like your job, find a way to make it better, or get out – find another one, find another career – you can find what will make you happy.

Much time has passed since my sister told me, when I was 28, that I was going to be an old maid if I didn't get married soon. Even today's role models on TV are married later. I think in particular of the show Friends, whose characters are single past 30, even 35. Today there is a choice as to whether to marry or not. It is a choice for you to consider seriously.

When I was 40 years old, I felt strong enough to say I wanted (needed) a commitment from my partner. When I was younger, even though I wished for a commitment, which was shown dramatically to me when my boyfriend started cheating on me, I was afraid to come right out and say "I want to know where this relationship is going. I am looking for a commitment and I need to know if that is what you want." Luckily, when I was ready to say that, my husband showed up, who was also ready for a commitment. After age 40, I also knew more of what I wanted in a partner. First of all, looks and a great body didn't matter so much any more. I found out that I could be attracted to a man who was kind and had similar interests just as easily as I could be to someone who had a great body. I knew I wanted to settle down, in my case in a country setting. When I saw the concern my husband put into taking care of my ill father, I knew that that was a quality that I also needed. I knew I needed someone with a stable work history and who did not drink. When I was younger these qualities were not as important, but as I grew, I knew this is what I wanted, and if I didn't find a man who possessed these qualities, I was very happy to live alone. Actually, I was very happy living alone, I had friends and activities that kept me busy (but, I also enjoyed being home alone with my cats).

When people ask you why you are *not* married, turn to them and say "Why are you married?" Then, explain all the great things that are going on in your life and re-assure them that you will partner up when and if the right time comes. Do not be intimidated into marrying just because your family (and friends) says you should be. What is right for you is what is right in your heart. Remember that. Even if what feels right in your heart is to go work in the Peace Corps in Africa, then do it. Appreciate the love you have in your life from your friends, family and even your pets. Intimate love will come your way when the time is right.

Appendix A Single's Civil Rights by State

The following table lists states that have laws that bar discrimination against singles. Please refer to Chapter 1 for more information.

Mindful Note

For details about the law, go to your state government's web site.

State	Employment	Housing	Insurance	Credit
Alabama	no	no	no	no
Alaska	yes	yes	no	yes
Arizona	no	no	mortgage only	no
Arkansas	no	no	no	yes
California	yes	yes	some lines	yes
Colorado	no	yes	no	yes
Connecticut	yes	yes	no	yes
Delaware	yes	yes	no	no
Florida	yes	no	no	yes
Georgia	no	no	no	no
Hawaii	yes	yes	no	yes
Idaho	no	no	no	no
Illinois	yes	yes	no	yes
Indiana	teachers only	no	no	no

State	Employment	Housing	Insurance	Credit
Iowa	no	no	no	no
Kansas	no	no	yes	no
Kentucky	no	no	no	no
Louisiana	no	no	no	yes
Maine	no	no	no	yes
Maryland	yes	yes	no	yes
Massachusetts	no	yes	no	no
Michigan	yes	yes	no	yes
Minnesota	yes	yes	no	yes
Mississippi	no	no	no	no
Missouri	no	no	yes	yes
Montana	yes	yes	group plans	yes
Nebraska	yes	yes	no	no
Nevada	no	no	no	yes
New Hampshire	yes	yes	some lines	no
New Jersey	yes	yes	no	yes
New Mexico	no	no	no	no
New York	yes	yes	no	yes

Appendix A Single Civil Rights by State

State	Employment	Housing	Insurance	Credit
North Carolina	no	no	no	yes
North Dakota	yes	yes	no	yes
Ohio	no	no	no	yes
Oklahoma	no	no	no	yes
Oregon	yes	yes	no	no
Pennsylvania	no	no	yes	no
Rhode Island	no	yes	no	yes
South Carolina	no	no	no	no
South Dakota	no	no	no	no
Tennessee	no	no	no	yes
Texas	no	no	no	no
Utah	no	no	no	no
Vermont	no	yes	no	yes
Virginia	yes	yes	yes	yes
Washington	yes	yes	some	no
West Virginia	no	no	no	no
Wisconsin	yes	yes	no	yes
Wyoming	no	no	no	no

State	Employment	Housing	Insurance	Credit
Total states with protections	20 yes, 1 teachers only	23 yes	4 yes, 5 some lines	27 yes

Appendix B Mortgage Worksheet

Use this worksheet as a tool to compare mortgage lenders that you have researched according to the directions presented in Chapter 2.   Make copies if you want to compare more than two lenders.

Mindful Note

Don't worry if you can't fill in all the fields for each lender, just complete as much information as you can, and compare from there.

	Lender 1		Lender 2	
Name of Lender				
Name of Contact				
Date of Contact				
Mortgage Amount				
Basic Information on the Loans	Mortgage 1	Mortgage 2	Mortgage 1	Mortgage 2
Type of Mortgage: Fixed rate, adjustable rate, conventional, FHA, other? If adjustable, see below.				
Minimum down payment required				
Loan term (length of loan)				

	Lender 1		Lender 2	
Name of Lender				
Contract interest rate				
Annual percentage rate (APR)				
Points (may be called loan discount points)				
Monthly Private Mortgage Insurance (PMI) premiums				
How long must you keep PMI?				
Estimated monthly escrow for taxes and hazard insurance				
Estimated monthly payment (Principal, Interest, Taxes, Insurance, PMI)				
Fees Different institutions may have different names for some fees and may charge different fees. We have listed some typical fees you may see on loan documents.				
Application fee or Loan processing fee				
Origination fee or				

Appendix B Mortgage Worksheet

	Lender 1		Lender 2	
Name of Lender				
Underwriting fee				
Lender fee or Funding fee				
Appraisal fee				
Attorney fees				
Document preparation and recording fees				
Broker fees (may be quoted as points, origination fees, or interest rate add-on)				
Credit report fee				
Other fees				
Other Costs at Closing/Settlement				

Title search/Title Insurance
    For lender
    For you				

Estimate prepaid amounts for interest, taxes, hazard insurance, payments to escrow				
State and local taxes, stamp taxes, transfer taxes				

	Lender 1		Lender 2	
Name of Lender				
Flood determination				
Prepaid Private Mortgage Insurance (PMI)				
Surveys and home inspections				
Total Fees and Other Closing/Settlement Cost Estimates				
Other Questions and Considerations about the Loan				
Are any of the fees or costs waivable?				
Prepayment penalties				
Is there a prepayment penalty?				
If so, how much is it?				
How long does the penalty period last? (for example, 3 years? 5 years?)				
Are extra principal payments allowed?				

Appendix B Mortgage Worksheet

	Lender 1		Lender 2	
Name of Lender				
Lock-ins				
Is the lock-in agreement in writing?				
Is there a fee to lock-in?				
When does the lock-in occur - 0 at application, approval or another time?				
How long will the lock-in last?				
If the rate drops before closing, can you lock-in at a lower rate?				
If the loan is an adjustable rate mortgage:				
What is the initial rate?				
What is the maximum the rate could be next year?				
What are the rate and payment caps each year and over the life of the loan?				
What is the frequency of rate change and of any changes to the monthly payment?				

	Lender 1		Lender 2	
Name of Lender				
What is the index that the lender will use?				
What margin will the lender add to the index?				
Credit life insurance				
Does the monthly amount quoted to you include a charge for credit life insurance?				
If so, does the lender require credit life insurance as a condition of the loan?				
How much does the credit life insurance cost?				
How much lower would your monthly payment be without the credit life insurance?				
If the lender does not require credit life insurance, and you still want to buy it, what rates can you get from other insurance providers?				

Appendix C Desired Partner Qualities Worksheet

Use this worksheet in conjunction with the information presented in Chapter 4 as a tool to decide the qualities you are looking for in a partner.   Place a checkmark in the box next to the indicated quality that most represents the level of importance for you.

Mindful Note

Refer to this table each time you meet someone new. Ask yourself: "Does this person have the qualities that are important to me."

Use the following key when rating your potential partner's qualities:

- Very Important: This is a quality that your partner MUST possess. There is no way you will become involved with someone who does not have this quality.

- Important: It is important that your partner possess this quality, but it is not necessary, especially if they have many qualities that you rated Extremely Important.

- No Opinion: You have no opinion as to whether your partner possesses this quality.

- Must Not Have: It is very important that your partner does not posses this quality.

Mindful Note

Also, before completing this table, clear your head and heart by performing the General Relaxation and Affirmations described in Chapter 5 of this book.   By being completely relaxed and confident you will get in touch with who you really are and what you really want.

Very Important	Important	No Opinion	Must Not Have	
How do you want your partner to prioritize their life?				
				Freedom / Casual Relationship
				Love/Relationship
				Work
				Arts/Hobbies
				Family
				Money
				Politics
				Intellectual culture
				Spirituality
What personality qualities are you looking for?				
				Sincerity and faithfulness
				Sobriety and/or moderation
				Cheerfulness and funny
				Creativity and a sense of art
				Generosity and kindness
				Public-spirited and refinement
				Willpower and courage
				Simplicity and naturalness

Very Important	Important	No Opinion	Must Not Have	
				Common sense and logic
				Beauty
				Even-temperedness
				Interested in having children soon
				Well-read
				Easy to talk to
				Professional
				Well-spoken
				Well educated
				Reliable
				Responsible
What do they do for fun?				
				Play music
				Paint
				Go to movies
				Go to the theater
				Read
				Dance
				Watch videos

Very Important	Important	No Opinion	Must Not Have	
				Take long walks
				Highly athletic activities
				Other
				Other
				Other

What characteristics would most annoy you?

				Anti-social
				Possessive or jealous
				Lazy
				A workaholic
				A sports fanatic
				Too money-conscious
				Quick to anger
				Promptness/Lateness

What would you like their Life Style to be like?

				Suburbs/City
				House/Apartment
				Active Easy (movies, shopping)
				Active Athletic

Very Important	Important	No Opinion	Must Not Have	
				Stay at Home
				Types of Movies
				Housework Division
				Working Partners
				Close Extended Family

Index

Index

Resources

[i] National Vital Statistics Report, Volume 51,Number 5 March 14,2003 *Deaths: Preliminary Data for 2001* by Elizabeth Arias, Ph.D., and Betty L. Smith, B.S. Ed., Division of Vital Statistics

[ii] http://www.gendercenter.org/mdr.htm

[iii] House Committee on Ways and Means Statement of Walter Welsh, Americans for Secure Retirement May 19, 2005

[iv] http://www.nber.org/aginghealth/spring03/w9782.html

[v] ORES Working Paper Series Number 89 *Widows Waiting to Wed? (Re)Marriage and Economic Incentives in Social Security Widow Benefits* Michael J. Brien Stacy Dickert-Conlin David A. Weaver Division of Economic Research January 2001

[vi] http://www.divorceinfo.com/survival.htm

[vii] http://www.gendercenter.org/mdr.htm

[viii] U.S. Census Bureau U.S. Department of Commerce May 2004 *Unmarried and Single Americans Week*

[ix] Homosexual Demography: Implications for the Spread of AIDS Journal of Sex Research, Nov, 1998 by Christopher Hewitt

[x] U.S. Census Bureau, American Community Survey *Unmarried-Partner Households in the United States: Description and Trends 2000 to 2003* Online at http://www.census.gov/acs/www/Downloads/3

[xi] Merck Manual of Aging: Online at http://www.merck.com/pubs/mmanual_ha/sec4/ch63/ch63h.html

[xii] McWhirter, David P. and Andrew M. Mattison. (1984) *The Male Couple: How Relationships Develop*. Englewood Cliffs, N.J.: Prentice-Hall.

[xiii] U.S. Census Bureau, American Community Survey 2002-2003, Census Supplementary Survey 2000-2001

[xiv] Ditto Page 8

[xv] U.S. Census Bureau U.S. Department of Commerce U.S. *Adults Postponing Marriage*, Census Bureau Reports June 29, 2001

[xvi] U.S. Census Bureau U.S. Department of Commerce *Marital Status and Living Arrangements,* March 1994 Arlene Saluter

[xvii] U.S. Census Bureau U.S. Department of Commerce http://www.census.gov/Press-Release/www/marital.html

[xviii] National Vital Statistics Report Volume 52,Number 22 June 10,2004 Births, Marriages, Divorces, and Deaths: Provisional Data for 2003

[xix] U.S. Census Bureau U.S. Department of Commerce *Marital Status and Living Arrangements,* March 1994 Arlene Saluter

[xx] National Center for Disease Control and Prevention, *Cohabitation, Marriage, Marital Dissolution, and Remarriage:* United States,1988 Data from the National Survey of Family Growth by Kathryn A. London, Ph.D. Division of Vital Statistics

[xxi] U.S. Census Bureau U.S. Department of Commerce *Record Share of New Mothers in Labor Force,* October 24, 2000:

[xxii] U.S. Census Bureau U.S. Department of Commerce *Fertility of American Women: June 2002,* October 2003

[xxiii] U.S. Census Bureau U.S. Department of Commerce, *Age At First Marriage At Record High,* March 13, 1996 by Arlene Saluter

[xxiv] U.S. Census Bureau, American Community Survey 2002-2003, Census Supplementary Survey 2000-2001.

[xxv] AARP: *Out-of-Pocket Spending on Health Care by Women Age 65 and Over in Fee-for-Service Medicare* 1998 Projections

[xxvi] American Association of Single People www.unmarriedamerica.org/facts.html

[xxvii] National Center for Health Statistics, C. A, Bachrach and M. C. Horn: *Married and Unmarried Couples, United States,* 1982. Series 23, No. 15. DHHS Pub. No. (PHS) 87–1991, Public Health Service. Washington. U.S. Government Printing Office' July 1987

[xxviii] American Association of Single People www.unmarriedamerica.org/facts.html

[xxix] www.dcu.com/streetwise/credit/

[xxx] Refer to the Federal Trade Commission's site for more information about obtaining a mortgage. http://www.ftc.gov/bcp/conline/pubs/homes/

[xxxi] Tennessee Housing Development Agency Online at: http://www.tennessee.gov/thda/Programs/Mortgage/undmort.html

Resources

---◇---

[xxxii] Federal Trade Commission Reverse Mortgages *Get the Facts Before Cashing In On Your Home's Equity* Online at: http://www.ftc.gov/bcp/conline/pubs/homes/rms.htm

[xxxiii] Federal Trade Commission: http://www.ftc.gov/bcp/conline/pubs/homes/bestmorg.htm

[xxxiv] http://www.contractors-license.org/ Provides licensing information for each of the 50 contiguous states. Also, find information on How to Find Out if a Contractor is Licensed

[xxxv] www.lawdepot.com contains a complete Service Agreement form. Even if you don't end up using this form, it can tell you the types of information that should go into it.

[xxxvi] Consumer Protection Division, Office of the Attorney General: http://www.atg.wa.gov/consumer/health.shtml#How

[xxxvii] All information in the Equal Credit Opportunity section was obtained from the national consumer protection web site. http://www.ftc.gov/

[xxxviii] Be sure to see a Financial Analyst or Bank Representative for assistance before investing your money. The information presented in this chapter is provided merely to help you get a high level familiarity with investment terms and procedures.

[xxxix] Choosing a Good Financial Advisor By J.D. MacRae, CFP http://www.networkingtoday.on.ca/articles/afinanc.htm

[xl] Most references described in this document can be found on the internet.

[xli] http://www.widowsource.com/Sex&Dating_content.html

[xlii] Divorce Info. Online at http://www.divorceinfo.com/dating.htm

[xliii] Dallas Morning News. Online at: http://www.egyptology.com/niankhkhnum_khnumhotep/dallas.html

[xliv] Stages of Gay Relationship Development. Online at: http://www.psychpage.com/gay/library/gay_lesbian_violence/stages_gay_relationships.html

Made in the USA
Lexington, KY
18 May 2012